"Girlfriends, get ready for a hilarious, but deeply insightful ride on this wonderful book bus. Whether married or single, you'll discover that Michelle's insights into Eden may forever change the way you look at yourself as a woman. With uncanny wisdom, you'll see yourself as whole and complete and beloved by God, whatever marital state you happen to be in."

BECKY FREEMAN, MARRIAGE COLUMNIST, SPEAKER, AND AUTHOR OF
MARRIAGE 911 AND *CHOCOLATE CHILI PEPPER LOVE*

"*If Men Are Like Buses* thoroughly and biblically answers the number-one question I'm most frequently asked by singles around the country. With tremendous insight, self-disclosure, and humor, Michelle teaches singles how to find fulfillment and love during their season of singleness."

DR. DON RAUNIKAR, PSYCHOLOGIST, SPEAKER,
AND AUTHOR OF *CHOOSING GOD'S BEST*

"Hop on the bus for a joyride through singlehood with Michelle McKinney Hammond in her inspirational new book, *If Men Are Like Buses*. If only this book had been available when we were single, we would have saved ourselves a lot of fretting while we waited for God to bring us together! Michelle reminds us that God will get us where we are supposed to go…eventually, in His perfect time!"

SUSAN WALES, AUTHOR OF *A MATCH MADE IN HEAVEN, BOOKS I AND II* AND
KEN WALES, EXECUTIVE PRODUCER OF *CHRISTY*

Other Books by Michelle McKinney Hammond

What To Do until Love Finds You
Secrets of an Irresistible Woman
The Genius of Temptation
His Love Always Finds Me
The Power of Femininity
Get a Love Life

IF MEN ARE LIKE BUSES,

Then How Do I Catch One?

Michelle McKinney Hammond

Multnomah® Publishers *Sisters, Oregon*

IF MEN ARE LIKE BUSES, THEN HOW DO I CATCH ONE?
Published by Multnomah Publishers, Inc.

© 2000 by Michelle McKinney Hammond
International Standard Book Number: 1-57673-691-1

Cover illustration by Milton Kingensmith
Cover design by Chris Gilbert

Unless otherwise marked, Scripture references are from *The Holy Bible,*
New International Version, © 1973, 1984 by the International Bible Society,
used by permission of Zondervan Publishing House.

Scripture references marked NASB are from the *New American Standard Bible,*
© 1960, 1977. by the Lockman Foundation.

Scripture references marked NLT are from the *Holy Bible,* New Living
Translation, © 1996. Used by permission of Tyndale House Publishers, Inc.
All rights reserved.

Multnomah is a trademark of Multnomah Publishers, Inc.,
and is registered in the U.S. Patent and Trademark Office.
The colophon is a trademark of Multnomah Publishers, Inc.

Printed in the United States of America

FOR INFORMATION:
Multnomah Publishers, Inc.•Post Office Box 1720•Sisters, Oregon 97759

Library of Congress Cataloging-in-Publication Data
McKinney Hammond, Michelle, 1957–
  If men are like buses, then how do I catch one? / by Michelle McKinney
Hammond.   p.cm.   ISBN 1-57673-691-1
  1. Single women—Religious life. 2. Mate selection—Religious aspects—
Christianity. I. Title.
  BV4596.S5 M345 2000   248.8'432—dc21   99-050868
       04 05 06 07 – 10 9 8 7

To the one who truly is the wheel in the middle of the wheel in my heart.
Jesus, you are truly the Lover of my soul.

Alma Hopkins, this one is for you.
Thank you for insisting that I was a writer
and for knowing a good title when you hear one.
It's a good thing I didn't disagree!

CONTENTS

ACKNOWLEDGMENTS

To my new family at Multnomah. Thank you for the gift you've given me—the freedom to express myself!

Bill Jensen, you continue to bless and inspire me. I treasure you.

Penny Whipps, girl, you know you got me going! I love you. Thank you, thank you!

Holly Halverson, my editor, thank you for making me look good and sound intelligent! I believe God handpicked you for this one; therefore, I am honored to have you.

And of course, to all my sisters who keep me honest, you know who you are—thank you!

INTRODUCTION

Yeah girl, it's me again. I know you thought to yourself, *Well, gee, after writing* What to Do until Love Finds You *and* Secrets of an Irresistible Woman, *she's got to be fresh out of anything else to say to us about being single.* Not! I've always got something more to say, 'cause God's always got something more to say.

Plus, the countless letters I received from readers of my first two books just added fuel to the fire in my heart to reach out to singles who were caught up in the struggle of trying to juggle a joyful life with the desire for companionship. We all know what the final goal is for most of us—a God-given relationship with Mr. Oh-So-Right—but how to get there in one piece is always the big question. Trying to find the answer can distract us from maintaining happy, healthy lives. Okay, listen up! It is important to note here that happiness is not a destination; it is a journey. It's all in the way you travel. Hopefully this book will make your sojourn a little smoother.

So let's talk a little about the trip: what to do, what not to do, and when to do (or not do) it. Let's get honest with ourselves, with God, and with whoever else counts. But most of all, let's get free—free to embrace each and every day of our lives whether we have a mate or not! Life is for the living, and you should be living it up.

So let's get down, get funky, get real, and get on with it! And when we're finished, you're gonna be able to love like you've never been hurt and dance like nobody's watching. You know why? Because you're more fabulous than you know.

Michelle

I watched him as he casually
　　dropped it
　This my heart
　　flicking it to the wind
　　　like the ashes
　　　　of a cigarette that had lost its fire
　　I silently screamed
　　　sensing the danger of pain
　　moving to rescue it
　　　from its downward plummet
　　　I sensed the lateness of the hour
　　Gone was the opportunity
　　　　to run from rejection
　　　　the die had been cast
　　　the deed had been done
Without hesitation
　　　without thought
　　　　so happy was I to find a willing candidate
to stand guardian over my love
　　　　I abdicated my post as the keeper of my heart
　　　　　with no formal references
　　　　hiring an unworthy
　　　　　unqualified stranger
　　　Now sensing in afterthought
the value of that
which had been broken
　　　　the stinging realization
　　　　of what I had done
　　　　　rivaled my disappointment
　　　　as my tears
　　　　　washed away the last
　　　　　　shades of rose from my eyes

I realized
    the blame was all mine
       for I had left my heart
          in the wrong place....

PART ONE

THE RIGHT PLACE

ONE

GET OUT OF THE STREET

The LORD God said, "It is not good for the man to be alone."
GENESIS 2:18

EXCERPTS FROM MY JOURNAL

SEPTEMBER 1977

I need a man, want a man, dream a man, eat a man, drink a man, want a man so bad I can taste the fulfillment of love, like cravings for a rich dessert, it haunts me even after I've had a whole meal. I can't explain it, I just want it.... I just really, really want a man.

JANUARY 1978

I'm lonely, so lonely I don't have to peel an onion to cry. So lonely that frustration has become my first name. So lonely that depression is my middle name...and I'm gonna wallow in my desperation because I'm lonely...and that's as good an excuse as any for sitting around and feeling sorry for the way my life is going.

JUNE 1979

Mama told me, "There's an owner for every cloth in the store." Well, I'm ready to be bought. I've been sitting here with the same pretty pattern on my face for a long time and I'm beginning to fade, ya know? So my question is this, is anyone interested in a piece of fabric that's collected so much dust?

MARCH 1985

I have come to the conclusion that love is not a play, in my mind the true drama is that the only place a solo belongs is on an empty stage.

I have a confession to make. You might ask, "Could it be more embarrassing than what you just shared?" It all depends on how important honesty is to you. Although I am writing this book as an "expert" on contentment as an unmarried woman, I feel it is important to share with you that I was once a miserable single.

"No kidding!" you huff. I'm glad you're not surprised. Though it's impossible to ignore my lack of victory in the past, once I pressed past that difficult passage in my life, I'm happy I never developed convenient amnesia about how painful being an unfulfilled single can be. It keeps me humble. It keeps me connected with reality—and with you. If you're truly honest with yourself, while reading my intimate journal ramblings you were either saying, "Po' thang!" or "I can relate!" Either comment leads us to the same question: How do we end up in such a state over a man?

A man—such a potent pair of words. Those two words alone could set off a dialogue that would last throughout eternity. But right now we are dealing with an immediate need. Every woman longs for a fulfilling, committed relationship with someone who really, really loves her. We're talking about the kind of love that gives you a reason to get up in the morning, smile in the middle of the afternoon, and laugh at the abuse that the world dishes out on a day-to-day basis.

But what if that relationship isn't immediate? What if it appears to be stalled somewhere between here and "happily ever after"? What then?

I'm here to tell you, you can be happy and single. I know—I have truly evolved from the woman who wrote those painful admissions in her journal. I am now, as a magazine article recently put it, sassy, single, and satisfied! "You mean the words 'single and satisfied' can coexist?" you ask. Yes indeed, and I am a personal witness!

"But," you interrupt, "I don't want to be happy and single, Michelle. I bought this book because I want a man!"

Hold on, I'm getting there! But before that relationship can come along, understand that some things have to be in place— mainly you.

Someone once said, "Men are like buses. If you miss one there's always another one coming around the corner." I would like to add to that. If you didn't learn anything when the first bus passed you by, what makes you think you'll catch the next one? I think we need to back up and approach the corner correctly. Therefore, we're not going to start with the man; we're going to start with you.

In order to catch the right bus—believe me, you can catch the wrong one—you've got to be in the right place, at the right time, doing the right thing. That's the point of this book. So if you don't mind, I'm going to take my time and drop a few things in your universe to get you on your way. Take a deep breath and repeat after me, "I'm ready for this; I'm ready for this; I'm ready for this." No need to click your heels three times because we're not going to Kansas; we're simply going to take a little journey back to the Garden of Eden to find out how this whole relationship mess began.

IN SEARCH OF EDEN

Once upon a time there was a girl named Evelyn. Now Evelyn had this really wealthy Father who set her up in royal fashion. She was proud to say she had a great relationship with her indulgent Daddy and never wanted for anything. He had even found the perfect mate for her. Why, Evelyn and this man were so compatible, being with him was like being with herself—they were true soul mates. Her Father had chosen well.

He always chose well—that's why she had no problem with being obedient to his instructions. That is, until she met Sly. Sly was, well, slick, smooth, and sly! He made suggestions that made Evelyn's toes tingle. He liked to walk on the wild side. Suddenly Evelyn became aware of things she never considered before. What Sly suggested made a whole lot of sense. Why should she listen to everything her Father said? She should be able to make some decisions on her own. Do her own thing. Be lord of her own destiny. Make up her own mind! After all, she was "grown" (that's urbanese for "an adult"). Life was a bowl of fruit, and she wanted to taste all of it.

As a matter of fact, she didn't mind sampling the piece Sly now dangled so invitingly in front of her. She hesitated for a brief second. *Hmm,* she thought, *maybe I shouldn't.... This is the one thing my Father told me to avoid.*

Oh, pooh, she decided, *he gave me everything else I wanted—he couldn't possibly get that upset about my tasting this one tiny piece of a delectable treat. After all, didn't he cultivate this very fruit in his own private garden?*

Crunch! Ooh, it was delicious! Evelyn handed it to her loving mate because they shared everything. The moment he swallowed the last bite, Evelyn knew something was wrong. Sly had slithered off in the middle of their taste test, and her honey was looking funny. Oh, no! She was looking funny too! She was naked! How long had she been parading around, ignorant of this embarrassing fact? And with this realization the frantic couple ran for cover.

And just when they thought things couldn't get any worse, they did—Father was heading their direction. How were they going to explain this mess? *Father won't punish me,* Evelyn comforted herself. *After all, it wasn't my fault….*

Sound a little familiar? Yup! You guessed it: The longing for love began with Adam and Eve when they plummeted into disobedience. Their mistake, which God called *sin,* set in motion a generational curse that few have recognized. That disastrous chain of events remains unbroken today, visiting every descendant of Adam and Eve on the face of the earth.

Today we are going to uncover the trick that Satan plays on us all. Since it is the truth that makes us free, that equips us to make choices that secure our liberty, I am going to tell you the truth. We are going to get to the root of why so many struggle with their singleness.

Singleness is not a curse. The misery many suffer as singles and the bad choices that misery provokes are, however. Therefore we need to get past this once and for all. Now I realize you know the story, but I want you to take another look at what *really* happened in the Garden. I want to talk about the stuff that nobody points out to us. Admittedly it's a beautiful study on the Creation, but there's a whole lot more going on in this tidy little presentation of how the world got started. So indulge me.

EDEN 101

In the beginning God existed in all his forms: God, the Word which became manifest in the form of Jesus, and the Holy Ghost.

And the three were one. Now, don't get stuck here. We don't want to tackle a deeper study on the Trinity right now—I'm trying to take us somewhere, so come along.

In the beginning, God created the world, the solar system, everything pertaining to life and godliness, and then he decided all of this stuff was so gorgeous that there should be worshipers to enjoy and appreciate the creation and the Creator.

I can relate to that. Nothing warms my heart more than knowing that my books have blessed someone. That's not vanity, just a healthy, God-given desire to be appreciated for a job you worked hard at.

Anyway, God discussed this with Jesus and the Holy Spirit; they counseled among themselves and came up with a fabulous idea. "Then God said, 'Let us make man in our image, in our likeness'" (Genesis 1:26).

Notice the words *us* and *our*. The whole Trinity was in on the decision! They then made this magnificent creature whom we've all come to love and adore, even in the midst of deep frustration, called *man*. God made man from the earth, breathed the breath of life into him, then took him and put him in Paradise, namely, the Garden of Eden. From the beginning, notice, only God's hand could transport man from where he was into a more glorious existence. Remember that.

Now, man was created on purpose, *with* a purpose. Besides appreciating God and his handiwork, he had an assignment. "The LORD God took the man and put him in the Garden of Eden to work it and take care of it" (Genesis 2:15).

Once Adam got busy doing his job, God, being the gracious God that he is, made another corporate decision. "The LORD God said, 'It is not good for the man to be alone. I will make a helper suitable for him'" (Genesis 2:18).

Here is an important fact that must not be overlooked. *God* decided that Adam needed a mate. *Adam* didn't have a clue. He didn't turn to God and say, "Hey, you know, it's been real nice hanging out with you, but what else have you got? I've got needs, you know." No, he was into fellowshipping with God. His heart was full to overflowing with love for his Creator. He relished their time together. He rejoiced in the world that God had so generously spread before him. He found his fulfillment in fulfilling his God-ordained purpose. He felt no lack.

Imagine: Adam felt no void, no screaming empty spaces in his heart. All was well with his soul. The mate thing was totally God's idea.

It also behooves us to note that everything God does has a purpose. He decided that Adam needed a helper to assist him in performing his purpose on earth. And he needed this helper on two levels: spiritual and natural. In that order.

ALL ONE OR ALONE?

Let's face it: Adam wasn't really alone. The Lord himself came down—did you hear me? *The Lord came down,* daily, from heaven, to walk and talk with Adam in the cool of the evening. Adam had divine fellowship with God. I'll tell you what true aloneness is: the absence of God. That is the epitome of alone. So Adam was not alone in the way that we define aloneness. Still, Adam had no concept of being one with another. He was not acquainted with the concept of true intimacy. He wasn't even aware he should want oneness with someone. You see, Adam was a *reflection* of God. He was not *one with* God. The idea of relationship, interaction with a being just like himself, was foreign.

In order for Adam to reflect the image of God accurately in the earth, he had to be connected to another. This is where he needed a helper in the spiritual sense. He had to be one with someone, mirroring the oneness of God, the Son, and the Holy Spirit.

Without this experience, he could only go so far in his worship experience. He would never learn to reach beyond himself. He would be self-centered. And that would limit both his grasp and his appreciation of God.

God wanted Adam to come outside of himself to a higher place. God wanted Adam's worship experience to grow to another level of emotional closeness. Once he became one with another, he would understand afresh the beauty of deep relationship. This would enhance his life and enrich his worship.

Whew! That is potent stuff!

On the other hand, Adam needed a helper in the natural sense. God understood the need for partnership to get a job done. When God created the world, Jesus, the Word come to Life, the Holy Spirit, and Wisdom were present to partake in this magnificent inception.

In the beginning was the Word, and the Word was with God, and the Word was God. (John 1:1)

Now the earth was formless and empty, darkness was over the surface of the deep, and the Spirit of God was hovering over the waters. (Genesis 1:2)

I, wisdom, dwell together with prudence; I possess knowledge and discretion. I was there when he set the heavens in place, when he marked out the horizon on the face of the deep. Then I was the craftsman at his side. (Proverbs 8:12, 27, 30)

Though God was the leading character in this epic, he understood that "two are better than one, because they have a good return for their work" (Ecclesiastes 4:9). He also was aware what the power of agreement and the spoken word could create. Solomon acknowledged it: "Though one may be overpowered, two can defend themselves. A cord of three strands is not quickly broken" (Ecclesiastes 4:12). And Genesis tells us: "Now the whole world had one language and a common speech…. But the LORD came down to see the city and the tower that the men were building. The LORD said, 'If as one people speaking the same language they have begun to do this, then nothing they plan to do will be impossible for them'" (Genesis 11:1, 5–6).

A side note here: If you haven't gotten busy performing your God-ordained purpose, then you can't tell God you need help—right? If you're in a paralyzed state, putting your life on hold until God gives you your mate, let me pour this in your Kool-Aid: God knows you don't need help feeling sorry for yourself. My suggestion? Stop asking God, "Why am I alone?" and begin asking him, "Why am I here?" You don't need help until you're doing something that requires help. So get busy, sister!

Now we see that God had decided that Adam needed someone to help him comprehend the notion of intimacy, but also someone who would be specially designed and equipped to help him complete his assignment on the earth. But before God created woman, he did something very interesting.

> Now the LORD God had formed out of the ground all the beasts of the field and all the birds of the air. He brought them to the man to see what he would name them; and whatever the man called each living creature, that was its name. So the man gave names to all the livestock, the birds of the air and all the beasts of the field.
>
> But for Adam no suitable helper was found. (Genesis 2:19–20)

Isn't that interesting? Why do you suppose God had Adam name the animals before he gave him a mate? This was a test. Had Adam really learned the heart of God? Did he truly walk in agreement with him? Did he call things as God saw them? Or did he just do his own thing? Since Adam's job was to maintain order in the earth, God gave him the authority to carry out this responsibility. He gave him the same power of the spoken word that God himself possessed. This was a major promotion. Adam was officially a partner with God! Therefore it was imperative that Adam become an extension of God's arm by being in one accord with him. Utilizing his authority apart from God could have serious consequences.

We must take note, however, that whether Adam was in agreement with God or not, whatever Adam called the animals was what they were going to be because he was a free agent. But Adam passed the test. He named the animals and agreed that none was a suitable prospect for partnering with him.

Now this is where some of us get messed up. We get stuck in the animal kingdom. In our search for a mate we name some animals the wrong thing. We fail to see some of the frogs and dogs we encounter for what they really are. We look past the obvious in our desperation for a partner and call whomever we meet "Mr. Right." And because God doesn't hold up his hand and scream "Stop!" we decide that this man, who everyone else can see is a poor choice, is the other half of a match made in heaven.

The truth of the matter is, if you don't invite God into the process of making your choice, he will allow you to do your own thing. He will let you name the animals as you see them and deal with the heartbreaking consequences. After all, you too are a free agent.

So, you see, Adam had some sense. He saw the animals for what they were and left them alone. He didn't waste his time getting scratched up by the lion or tromped on by the elephant. He didn't try to make it work with the giraffe. He dusted off his hands and moved on. The man was still whole, still free, even though he had noticed that everything he named had a mate, a helper, of its own kind.

GIVE IT A REST

The story goes on to say that God caused a deep sleep to fall on Adam. Do you know that God will help you rest in him while you wait for your mate—if you let him? Adam didn't struggle with God. The Creator was his friend. He trusted him completely. This is what gave God room to move and make good determinations for Adam's life.

So while Adam slept, God went about creating a helper for Adam, one he knew Adam would like. She would be equipped with everything Adam needed to help him carry out his duties, yet come with features that would bring pleasure to him as well.

Have you ever had a secret fear that God would give you a mate you didn't find attractive or didn't like, even though he was "good" for you? Mmm-hmm, I've been there. Obviously that wasn't true in Adam's case. Notice that Adam didn't give God a list of what he liked, what he wanted, or even what he thought he deserved. He just went to sleep, leaving the choice to God.

This reminds me of when I was a little girl. Every time my mother served a new dish I would say, "I don't like that. I don't want to eat it." My dad always said, "You're too young to know what you like. How can you say you don't like what you haven't experienced?" Then he made me taste it. And sure enough, I liked it. You see, he knew something I didn't—it was *good*.

Well, God knows what we like. And he also knows what we need. If you haven't learned yet from your bad choices to let him do the picking, you can begin anytime. Every happily married couple I know *knew* it was God who brought them together. I think that says something.

And while he was sleeping, [God] took one of the man's
ribs and closed up the place with flesh. Then the LORD
God made a woman from the rib he had taken out of the
man, and he brought her to the man.

The man said,

"This is now bone of my bones and flesh of my flesh;
she shall be called 'woman,' for she was taken out of
man." (Genesis 2:21–23)

When God woke Adam and presented Eve to him, Adam didn't
need a formal introduction! He recognized immediately that this
was his missing piece. Adam confirmed his oneness with her and
acknowledged that indeed she was part of him. She was to be his
woman, his wife, joined to him forever.

Now, ladies, I know that you are hip and all, but take a lesson
from Eve. She did not walk up to Adam and flirt with him. She did
not run over to where he was sleeping, tap him on the shoulder,
and say "Hey! God said that you were my husband!" No, no, no!
She allowed God to present her to him and she allowed Adam to
recognize her as God's choice and gift.

Many of you think you have to help a man realize that you are
the one. Not so. God puts that knowledge in the heart of a man.
For you to jump-start the relationship is severely out of order. Even
if you succeed, you will have problems later.

While you're wondering why the man in your life won't wake
up and smell the coffee concerning your place in his life, let me
pose this question to you: When did Adam wake up? My lovely
friend, the answer is (can I get a drum roll?): *when Eve was finished.*
Are you finished becoming all that God wants to make and mold
you to be? How can you know the man you've selected fits in God's
plan for your life if you don't know what that plan is? Give it some
thought.

You see, only after God has completed his work in preparing you will you be truly ready to receive the person he wants to add to your life. Obviously here I'm talking to those who truly desire God's choice and not their own for their lives. Let's face it—we could all be married if we just wanted to be married. But to be married to the right person, God's chosen best for you, you have to let him make the choice *and* decide when you're ready to receive it.

Adam allowed God to prepare him and decide what exactly he needed. He waited upon God's good and perfect design.

The Word continues: "The man and his wife were both naked, and they felt no shame" (Genesis 2:25). Adam and Eve were not self-conscious because they were totally God-conscious. God had been the first and only other person to touch them both. Therefore they could stand before one another and God with nothing to hide. They were vulnerable in their nakedness, yet felt no threat to their well-being.

Adam and Eve were transparent in their appreciation of one another, as well, because they were virgins in every sense. Their consciences were free. They had no baggage from past mistakes. They could be totally open because all they had to show was what God had put there. And everything that God had placed within them was "good."

But then something bad happened. Eve had an encounter that would change their lives forever. She fell for the serpent's line that God was withholding something from her—"equal rights," he said. Even back in B.C. those words were enough to stir up a hornets' nest of trouble. The willful woman rose up in her, convincing her she deserved to be as knowledgeable as God. Why should he be the only one to know everything? So she took the fruit and ate it and gave it to Adam as well.

Now Adam had really gotten into this new concept of oneness, so in the interest of remaining one with Eve, he also took the fruit and ate it. That's when the whole love story took a turn for the worse. Now the "perfect couple" had something to hide. Shame was a new feeling and not a pleasant one. Since Adam and Eve had chosen to know good and evil, the first thing they knew was that they were naked. Suddenly they were overwhelmed with self-conciousness. As they scrambled to hide from God, who was rapidly approaching, the concept of oneness was shattered, and suddenly it was every man for himself and every woman for herself.

WHERE ARE YOU?

The Word then tells us, "But the LORD God called to the man, 'Where are you?'" (Genesis 3:9). Now, do you think for one moment that God didn't know where Adam was? Puh-leeze! Adam was the one in the dark. Hiding behind the curtain of his own disobedience, he didn't realize he had literally snatched his heart out of God's hands and claimed his life as his own. Adam had decided to become his own source. When Adam and Eve made the choice to seek the knowledge of good and evil for themselves, they canceled God's presence out of the picture.

Too bad. They could have taken a shortcut by asking God anything they wanted to know and have stayed in his good graces. Instead they swallowed a lie, hook, line, and sinker, only to be caught on the end of the line by God himself. That was too much responsibility for Adam to bear.

> The man said, "The woman you put here with me—she gave me some fruit from the tree, and I ate it."
> Then the LORD God said to the woman, "What is this you have done?"
> The woman said, "The serpent deceived me, and I ate." (Genesis 3:12–13)

The man blamed the woman. The woman blamed the serpent. And the serpent? Well, he had nowhere to place the blame except on his own hate-filled heart, so he didn't even bother to explain. And here is the point that I have been leading up to all this time. The reason we go through so much angst when it comes to relationships and the longing for a mate can be found in the following statements.

To the woman he said,
"[Because you have done this,] I will greatly increase your pains in childbearing;
with pain you will give birth to children.
Your desire will be for your husband, and he will rule over you."

To Adam he said,
"Because you listened to your wife and ate from the tree about which I commanded you, 'You must not eat of it,'
Cursed is the ground because of you;
through painful toil you will eat of it all the days of your life.
It will produce thorns and thistles for you,
and you will eat the plants of the field.
By the sweat of your brow you will eat your food until you return to the ground." (Genesis 3:16–19)

What was God saying? Let me break it down for you. This has been one of the most misused portions of Scripture ever. Many a man has used Genesis 3:16 to build a case for submission. This is not a submission Scripture. This pronouncement from God details the state of the fallen heart and the consequences it bears in that condition. You must understand that though God cursed the serpent, he did not curse the man or the woman directly. Instead their ability to be fruitful *apart from him* was cursed.

Fruitfulness, whether it is in reference to a woman's having children or to a man's being successful in his career, has always been a source of validation in society. It separates the boys from the men, the women from the girls, in the minds of many. Down through the ages, this ability to be fruitful has had major significance. To not achieve fulfillment in family or career meant you were disregarded or forsaken by God. This is the epitome of a curse—to be held in contempt, separated from and ignored by God. It all started that fateful day in the Garden.

This punishment, or curse, affected all women, not just married women. It affected all men, not just married men. After doing research of the original text, I discovered that what God was basically saying to Eve was, "Since you have turned your heart away from me, you will be ruled by your desire for fulfillment from another source. And you will be disappointed because man is incapable of being the source that I am."

This is why single women struggle with being single and why many a married woman still struggles for contentment. No *man* can fill all the empty spaces in your world. According to the curse, women would spend all their time, energy, and emotion seeking affirmation and fulfillment from men but never getting it because it was not men's to give.

Therefore the woman would be ruled by her desire to have a man complete, validate, and affirm her. Her ability to cultivate a fruitful relationship with man apart from God would be difficult. And furthermore, no man would be able to save woman from her pain. *Healing and wholeness are in the hands of God alone.*

Mm-mm-mm. Are you getting this? This is important. This is the first major key to catching that bus, girl! Now that we've located the root of this longing-for-a-man business, you've got to nip this curse in the bud in your own life; get your eyes off of the bus; and get connected to the Person who controls the bus route.

As for the man, poor, poor dear, he didn't escape either. Originally God had made it easy for Adam to provide for the woman. As long as Adam was plugged into God, the ground gave up lush crops without his having to strain a muscle. But since Adam had taken the provision of God for granted, Eve would now get to see him sweat. He would learn there was a big difference between tending to God's ever-ready creation and compelling it to grow. The ground would no longer cooperate with him. Shoot, Eve wouldn't either, for that matter. Everything around Adam would now be at odds with him.

No wonder men feel as if everybody is giving them a hard time—everybody is! It is only as we keep our hearts turned toward God for all we need that provision flows in abundance, minus the struggle. Before, Adam was hardly working, but now he was going to have to work hard—work hard to eat; work hard to gain the woman's respect; work hard to be fruitful. Now Adam had to toil to exercise dominion, to subdue, and to maintain order in his world. Adam's role was switched from that of supervisor to laborer.

Since Adam and Eve wanted to be like God, apart from God, they would now see that they couldn't handle God's job. There was only one God, and he would not share his glory, the ability to be the source of all things, with another. He had given man the authority to be his representative on the earth. But as we all know, a representative is merely that; he does not replace the one he represents.

From the beginning, man and woman were never designed to be each other's source of fulfillment. They were designed to be companions and working partners. They were to reflect God's care for them by the way they cared for one another. Adam was supposed to lead and protect Eve, while sharing with her all that he had learned from God. Eve was to be a reflection of all that Adam imparted to her and the conduit to his completing the tasks the Lord had set before him.

Adam had failed miserably in his charge. He had allowed Eve to be deceived by the serpent. He did not exercise his God-given authority over the situation. Instead he joined in her folly. God was not upset because Adam literally listened to Eve. After all, God had created her to be a helper to him. That indicates she would have wise suggestions to offer as she assisted Adam. His mandate as Eve's covering was to review all suggestions in the light of God's Word before making a decision. No, it was the fact that Adam internalized what she said and acted upon it against his better judgment. God couldn't let that slide. Adam had to learn there was a price to be paid for his disobedience toward God and the shirking of his responsibilities toward the woman.

Eve, though she was deceived, had to be punished as well because disobedience to God is serious. So much for that famous line we love to throw out when we're sliding around on his grace: "God knows my heart." Yes, he does, but because he can't go against his own law, our actions still bear their consequences. Why? To break it down even further: Your actions reveal where your heart *truly* is. The flesh follows the heart's suggestions.

Ladies, it's time to get off the street of relying upon man for fulfillment and get back to the Garden of God's generous provision. To remain on the street is to fulfill one very scary prophecy. Listen to Isaiah: "In that day seven women will take hold of one man and say, 'We will eat our own food and provide our own clothes; only let us be called by your name. Take away our disgrace!'"(Isaiah 4:1).

Here the prophet warns what will happen to Israel if it continues to rebel against God and seek other forms of fulfillment: Desperation will take over. Is that frightening or what? Yet we see it happening all around us. Just tune in to any daytime talk show. The curse is in effect, big-time!

Why are we so hung up on acquiring a man's name to validate our womanhood? I'll tell you why. The Word tells us, "Adam named his wife Eve, because she would become the mother of all the living" (Genesis 3:20). Before the Fall, woman had simply been called "woman" because she was taken out of man. According to Dake's Annotated Reference Bible, since *Adam* without the definite article means *man,* woman was "womb-man," or "man with a womb." I kind of get a picture of them both answering when God called, so tight was their oneness. But after the Fall, their relationship changed. Their willfulness had severed their oneness. God had to restore their unity. He now would have to be the third cord that would keep them together. Yet God allowed Adam to reinforce the fact that the authority structure had not changed in spite of their disobedience. He was still responsible for the woman. It would still be the man's job to name things. It would still be the woman's job to partner with him in all that he had been instructed to do before. So Adam bestowed a name upon Eve that would be a prophetic blessing. And women have been looking for a man to give them a name, to define them and establish their sense of purpose, ever since.

BACK TO THE GARDEN

Though the man and woman would eventually die, it was an act of mercy on God's part to expel Adam and Eve from the Garden lest they then partake of the tree of life and be forever bound in the sad state they had brought upon themselves. As God guided them out of the Garden and into the world they had unconsciously chosen, I find his purpose for them most interesting. The Word says:

"So the LORD God banished him from the Garden of Eden to

work the ground from which he had been taken" (Genesis 3:23).

Notice God still saw Adam and Eve as one—the Scripture says both were put out of the Garden—yet they no longer saw each other that way through the haze of their sin. Another translation states that God sent Adam from the Garden "to cultivate the ground from which he was taken" (NASB). What can we learn from this? We might not feel that we are in an ideal situation as singles, but we are to deal with where we are, what we are made of, and work it! Work out our purpose, cultivate our relationship with God, and refine our lives right where we are.

"How is this possible?" you ask. "This whole thing is a mess! Is there any hope?"

Yes indeed: "Then Shecaniah son of Jehiel, one of the descendants of Elam, said to Ezra, 'We have been unfaithful to our God by marrying foreign women from the peoples around us. But in spite of this, there is still hope for Israel'" (Ezra 10:2). That about sums it up. Though we've gone looking for love and fulfillment in all the wrong places, there is still hope. There is hope because Jesus paved a path back to the Garden by going there first and praying for us. He asked his Father to reestablish the pipeline between us that we might become one again: one with God, one with one another. "I pray...for those who will believe in me...that all of them may be one, Father, just as you are in me and I am in you.... I have given them the glory that you gave me, that they may be one as we are one: I in them and you in me" (John 17:20–23).

Then Jesus took the curse, the consequence of the original sin, and nailed it to the tree as he hung dying for you and for me. When he rose from the dead, he handed us back the gift of authority and the keys to the kingdom that Adam and Eve dropped that day in the Garden. He restored us to our rightful place as God-ordained supervisors over the earth.

You see, Jesus came to clear up all of the confusion about who is the source of all the love, all the knowledge, all the power that we seek. He came to bring restoration to our relationships, wholeness to our hearts, fulfillment to our souls, and liberty to those held captive by the lies of the deceiver. And to top it all off, Jesus himself promises to give us a new name!

You will be called by a new name that the mouth of the LORD will bestow.

...No longer will they call you Deserted, or name your land Desolate.

But you will be called Hephzibah ["my delight is in her"], and your land Beulah ["married one"]. (Isaiah 62:2, 4)

So much for the name a man will give us—it's temporary at best. As we retrace Jesus' footsteps back to the Garden, we find the original source of love. As we tap into the source of true fulfillment and validation of all that we were created to be, a miraculous thing happens—we find contentment in whatsoever state we are in. We are once again naked and unashamed, lacking and wanting nothing. Never again will you feel the need to explain why you aren't married.

And by the way, contentment is the greatest beauty secret I know. Men can sniff desperation and neediness ten miles away, and believe me, once they get a whiff, they flee. When you are finally at peace with yourself, by yourself, get ready, 'cause when that bus comes around the corner and sees a fulfilled woman standing there, guess what? It's gonna stop whether you are waving or not!

Before that happens, I think we ought to pray.

Dear Heavenly Father, for as long as I can remember I've sought love and validation in all the wrong places. Please forgive me for ignoring your outstretched hands. Forgive me for rejecting the love you offer in exchange for mere temporal prizes. Help me to realize the depth of your love and care for me. Make it so real that I run to embrace you. Fill my heart with yourself and let your affections drown out the lies that lured me to go in the wrong direction.

Please heal my hurts as you begin to reveal to me where I went wrong. Help me to welcome the truth as my friend, knowing it is the truth that will make me free. By your Spirit, break the patterns of the past that have rendered me unvictorious and bound by my own desires.

As I commit my heart back into your hands, please keep it safe. I choose to trust you to be the source of all I need and crave. Accept me back into your arms as I bow before you now, choosing to begin again, afresh and anew in my love commitment to you.

I now invite you to be more than my Savior—be the Lover of my soul, my one true love, in Jesus' name. Amen.

TWO

DRESSING FOR THE JOURNEY

When the turn came for Esther...to go to the king, she asked for nothing other than what Hegai, the king's eunuch who was in charge of the harem, suggested. And Esther won the favor of everyone who saw her.

ESTHER 2:15

So now that we've exposed the root of our problem, let's continue working from the inside out. Let me ask you a few questions before we go any further. What do you think of yourself? How would you describe yourself to someone if you were being objective? Would *you* want to get to know you if you met yourself walking down the street? By now you should know what time it is. That's right, it's time to get under the skin you're in.

If you read my first book, *What to Do until Love Finds You*, you know I told the story of a man who had hurt me deeply—so deeply I had a tea party with the devil who served me Unbelief Tea and Resignation Pie topped with Why Me? Sauce. Well, here's the sequel. He got divorced. He became a Christian. He came back to me. We had a major disagreement. He married someone else without telling me. (Can you believe he got married on me twice?

What was I thinking?) Though it took a while, which is another story altogether, we resolved the past and today we're friends. We were having a discussion one day when I jokingly said, "Oh, no one wants to marry me."

To which he said, "Why wouldn't anyone want to marry you?"

To which I replied, "I don't know."

To which he came back with, "Yes, you do. Why wouldn't anybody want to marry you?"

That's when the light came on in my head. I really couldn't think of any reason why a man with good sense wouldn't want to marry me! (Actually, I think I had only said that to him to give him a jab of guilt for dumping me in the first place.) So I said, "You know, I'm think I am absolutely fabulous! I wasn't always fabulous, but I am now, so the reality is that a man would be a fool not to want to marry me because I am a complete package."

To which he replied, "Well, there you have it. I thought you knew that. You would be quite a catch for someone, but if you don't know it, no one else will either. And they will treat you accordingly."

Hmm. That caused me to pause and reflect. When my friend and I had that conversation, I hadn't even realized that lately I had been attracting a different kind of man. I had broken the cycle of disappointing relationships. What had changed? I had changed. That's when it clicked. *We attract people who feed off of what we think of ourselves.* Did you know that? When I felt I wasn't a great prize, I attracted people who reinforced that idea in my mind. I didn't feel beautiful inside or out, so I allowed them to make me feel unattractive. I didn't feel as if I had any personal purpose, so I would lose myself in theirs and neglect the call God had placed on my life. And after they left me and moved on, their arms filled with the things I had helped them to acquire, I watched them go, drowning in my own emptiness. Alone again, with nothing to show for it.

I wrote a pitiful song after one of these relationships called "Broken Pieces." Oh, what a dirge. It said,

I feel like crying but the tears won't come.
What's the use of trying when I know that you are gone?
You came and went and all that's left
Are broken pieces of my heart...
Just broken pieces of a discarded heart.
Broken pieces cut deep and leave their mark.
Broken pieces lying on the floor.
Broken pieces that can't be mended anymore....
That's the price of living when you love someone
So hard that you can't stop giving.
Guess I wasn't very smart.
You threw my heart against the wall,
And watched it breaking from the fall.

Are you feeling sorry for me yet? Oh, it gets worse.

Guess it doesn't matter.
It was just a heart to you.
An empty present that someone gave to you.
A nameless owner.
What am I supposed to do with broken pieces?

That was the key. I gave my heart away to the undeserving because I didn't know how much it was worth. I pawned it for temporary affection and blew my wad on a chance. Now I had no heart and no cash to get it back. I was empty, spent by my efforts to fulfill myself with external sources that would never satisfy.

Scripture says, "He who is full loathes honey, but to the hungry even what is bitter tastes sweet" (Proverbs 27:7). I don't think

I had any concept of what honey tasted like. It wasn't real to me. For me the bitter was as good as it got. It was what I was used to, therefore I decided I should settle for it. After all, some man was better than no man at all, right? Looking back, I see myself as this woman running around with her heart in her hand saying, "Take my heart, why don'tcha? Try it, you'll like it!" Well, who would consider a giveaway valuable?

Are you getting this? Consider what happens when you get serious about buying diamonds. Not costume jewelry, not cubic zirconias—I'm talking about serious diamonds, clear, white, no inclusions, no sulfur, no flaws, pure clarity, with a brilliant cut. You don't find those in the front room at the jeweler's. Mm-mm. The salesperson takes you to the back room. Then he or she goes to a vault, manipulates a combination, and takes out a box. Sitting down at a desk and putting on a light, the salesperson opens the box and pulls out a black-velvet tray. He or she then picks up an instrument made for handling stones, carefully selects a gem, and holds it up to the light for you to behold. This stone is for your eyes only. Every Tom, Dick, and Harry doesn't get to see this. It is presented to you and you alone because you are serious about making a purchase.

You are like that diamond. You are not for every man to behold, only the one who has serious intentions toward you. But if you don't know your own heart's value, you'll go and hang it out with the costume jewelry on the counter where there is easy access. It will gather fingerprints, and you will wonder why it hasn't been purchased.

Girl, it's time to know your worth and make no apologies for it.

MIRROR, MIRROR

How do we get to the place where our soul is full and our self-worth is intact? And how do we master confidence with grace?

After all, we don't want to get lost in our own wonderfulness and unconsciously repel that potential mate.

When I address self-confidence and self-worth, please understand that I'm not talking about this modern-day theology of being "full of self." This is only another term for selfish. Both leave you alone with you. Our lives should be comfortably hidden in Christ. Get rid of the opera-singer syndrome: There is no more space for "me, me, me." Your life is no longer about you, but about Christ who dwells in you.

I am talking about getting a healthy perspective of your worth as a woman through Christ. After all, you have a King for a fiancé! *Dahling!* You can't lower your standards to roll in the mud with mere commoners. There shall be no casting of your pearls before swine. But first you've got to get the understanding that you are a pearl of great price. Somebody died for you—namely Jesus. That's no small drop in the bucket. If he thought you were worth dying for, what makes you think others should abuse the life he went through so much to save?

It is important for us to see ourselves as the King sees us. This can be difficult when we are bombarded by so-called perfect images via the media. According to them we should all be a streamlined size six or eight. I don't know about you, but I haven't hit that number since high school. As we hear accounts of eating disorders, so many struggling to be the perfect size, I always wonder, *Gee, what kind of personality could she possibly have while she's starving herself?* I don't know about you, but I get downright evil when I'm hungry. That is, unless I'm fasting, because then I'm in the Spirit, don'tcha know.

Could it be that even the Shulammite woman in the Song of Songs suffered from peer pressure on beauty issues? Though she spoke with confidence to her friends in defense of her looks, she tended to lose that confidence when addressing the man of her dreams. She didn't proclaim her attributes to her loved one the way she did to her girlfriends. After all, every maiden in the country was in love with him. Why should he consider her? She had flaws. Wouldn't someone more perfect than she catch his attention?

> Dark am I, yet lovely,
>   O daughters of Jerusalem,
> dark like the tents of Kedar,
>   like the tent curtains of Solomon.
> Do not stare at me because I am dark,
>   because I am darkened by the sun.
> My mother's sons were angry with me
>   and made me take care of the vineyards;
>   my own vineyard I have neglected. (Song of Songs 1:5–6)

I'm sure her tan was gorgeous! And her wild hair was exotic. Surely King Solomon thought so. He went on to sing her praises and pay tribute to her beauty. Check this out and compare his evaluation to hers.

> How beautiful you are, my darling!
>   Oh, how beautiful!
> Your eyes behind your veil are doves.
> Your hair is like a flock of goats
>   descending from Mount Gilead.
> Your teeth are like a flock of sheep just shorn,
>   coming up from the washing.
>   Each has its twin; not one of them is alone.
> Your lips are like a scarlet ribbon;
>   your mouth is lovely.
> Your temples behind your veil are
>   like the halves of a pomegranate.

Your neck is like the tower of David,
>   built with elegance; on it hang a thousand shields,
>   all of them shields of warriors.
Your two breasts are like two fawns,
>   like twin fawns of a gazelle that browse among the lilies.
All beautiful you are, my darling;
>   there is no flaw in you. (Song of Songs 4:1–5, 7)

She doesn't sound like an unkept vineyard to me. My, my! When was the last time a man commented on your temples? This brother took in every detail of her. Despite this woman's own opinion of herself, this man thought she was all that and a bag of chips, okay?

"There is no flaw in you." Well, I'm telling you right now, the man who says that to me has got me for keeps! So despite sunburned skin and what she felt was her disheveled condition, he saw perfection. Why? How? He went on to explain exactly what it takes to get a king's attention. I think his dissertation reveals a lot of clues that we can use to our own love advantage.

You have stolen my heart, my sister, my bride;
>   you have stolen my heart with one glance of your eyes,
>   with one jewel of your necklace.
How delightful is your love, my sister, my bride!
>   How much more pleasing is your love than wine,
>   and the fragrance of your perfume than any spice!
Your lips drop sweetness as the honeycomb, my bride;
>   milk and honey are under your tongue.
The fragrance of your garments is like that of Lebanon.
You are a garden locked up, my sister, my bride;
>   you are a spring enclosed, a sealed fountain.
Your plants are an orchard of pomegranates with choice fruits.

> With henna and nard, nard and saffron,
> calamus and cinnamon,
> with every kind of incense tree,
> with myrrh and aloes and all the finest spices.
> You are a garden fountain,
> a well of flowing water streaming down from
> Lebanon. (Song of Songs 4:9–15)

Well, there's no denying the man had a serious rap! It's true men are moved by what they see, while women are moved by what they hear. And she got an earful. This brother covered her inside and out.

What's really important to a man? From his list, I think we've been misled by the media. It's not about looking like Catherine Zeta-Jones, Julia Roberts, or Halle Berry, though they are absolutely gorgeous. It's not about being model-thin with waist-length hair and chiseled cheekbones. It's about being a complete package. The outer wrapping should only cover even more magnificent contents. Though King Solomon commented on the Shulammite woman's outward appearance in great detail, I find it fascinating that the list of inner qualities was longer. Let's take a look at it all.

The first thing that arrested the king were the woman's eyes. He said that they were like doves, which signifies that she did not boldly come on to him; she didn't stare him down from across the room. She was smoother than that. She made a louder statement with her silence by displaying modesty and humility.

Let me add another note here. It has been said the eyes are the windows to the soul. This statement is not from Scripture, but it is true. If you are harboring any pain, any anger, any distrust, it will come to light in your eyes. It is important to clear your heart's deck with God so these negative things don't become deflectors when you look at others. Your lips can smile but your eyes will give your bitter heart away every time, and no amount of eye makeup can camouflage a wounded heart.

Let's see. He liked her hair. It was like goat's hair—soft, with texture, long and luminous. I love to experiment with hair. Women today have so many options that there is no excuse for not having beautifully groomed hair. You can go for short or for locks that sway in the breeze. If you don't have it naturally, then, by golly, you can buy it! Don't be above doing whatever it takes to get your head together—in more ways than one. Hair occasionally had significance in Scripture. For example, a Nazirite priest was not supposed to cut his hair. It was a sign of his commitment to God. What does your hair say about you?

Ooh, get this—he mentions her teeth! I can relate to this. I had braces when I was in high school. Call me supersensitive if you want to, but I do find myself checking out a man's mouth at our first meeting. I can't help it! Good, clean teeth are important. A bright, beautiful smile indicates careful grooming and hygiene— all the things you want to believe take place before you kiss that person.

I hope you don't feel I'm being too crass, but you bought this book because you wanted a man in your life, right? Well, I'm trying to clue you to what's important to a man. I'm your friend. I've got to tell the truth, so don't get bitter, get better. The king noted that her teeth were perfect—even and in line. Now, I know everyone doesn't have perfect teeth, but cleanliness goes a long way to fill in the gaps nature left vacant (no pun intended). Make that toothbrush fly, girl!

While the king was busy discovering his lover's mouth, he also noticed what came out of it. He said her speech was comely. She spoke things that were inviting, that caused him to want to spend time with her. And you thought men didn't listen. And he went further than that.

MY, WHAT LOVELY FRUITS YOU HAVE!

Her temples were like pomegranates. Here he again addressed modesty and perhaps the blush a good smile brings to the face. She was pleasant and approachable. Though she did not reach out to him, everything about her mannerisms drew him to her.

Her neck was elegant, erect with confidence and grace. It gave a quiet testimony of who she was. Her virtues were like a necklace, adorning her to be admired. And her breasts were like fawns, beautiful and quietly beckoning his touch.

The king moved on to her inner qualities, but I love how he revealed his heart to her. He called her his sister, his bride. That says a lot. Men are very protective of their sisters. He treasured her completely, he said; he would grant her the same consideration and protection he would give to a sister. She would be treated like a blood relative in his life.

But check out what else he said. The first thing he referenced again was her eyes. This is the second mention. Truly her countenance was of utmost importance to him. Every man seeks a woman he can trust. Therefore one who has suspicion and hostility written all over her face, as reflected in her eyes, will not be of interest to him.

In his beauty inventory the king mentioned the beauties of her lips and mouth. As for her lips, they dripped like the honeycomb, and milk and honey were under her tongue. (Well, I say! Am I old enough to be reading this? No wonder the Jews weren't allowed to read Song of Songs until they were thirty!) In other words, girl-friend's conversation was sweet to his ears. Her lips were a source of delectable delight as far as he was concerned. No sarcastic remarks, no demanding barbs, no words with an edge, nothing but nourishing goodness came from that mouth of hers. Think about what warm milk and honey will do to you: They will make you sleepy. Yup, her words were balm to him, soothing a weary soul.

Are you getting this? Your bus ride will last only as long as your pleasant conversation does. Develop the spirit of an exhorter.

Her love was delightful, he was saying; he looked forward to seeing her. Her presence was intoxicating to him. Even the fragrance of her garments filled him with delight. In other words, the fruit of the Spirit emanated from her inner being like a sweet perfume. It had him enraptured.

How did she have him so wrapped around her little finger? The answer is in his description. She was an enigma, a mystery yet to be discovered, a challenge yet to be captured, intriguing, tantalizing. How do we know this? Because she was, as he put it, "a locked garden," a "sealed fountain," an "enclosed spring." That's right. The woman kept her body to herself, under lock and key. Her body was for her husband only.

Just remember: When a man is thirsty, he will be willing to pay anything for a drink. But once he drinks for free, it's over. The opportunity to negotiate is lost until he gets thirsty again. As Mama used to say, "Why buy the cow if you can get the milk for free?" I say it this way: A parked bus is an empty bus. Give the man in your life something to reach for, and he'll keep driving toward your desired destination.

Notice the list of fruits he uses in praising her. They are significant. First of all, pomegranates were hung around the hem of the high priest's robe when he entered the Holy of Holies to worship before God—they were an important part of his priestly outfit (Exodus 39:25–26). Pomegranates were also used to make a very pleasant spiced wine.

And check out the spices. Nard, calamus, cinnamon, and myrrh were all used to make costly oils and perfumes or anointing oil. Henna and saffron were used as penetrating dyes. These two in particular did not fade easily—they got under the skin. Aloes are healing. Spices add flavor to everything they touch.

With all these flowering descriptions, what was the king saying? There was nothing cheap about this woman. Everything about her assaulted his senses. The "fruits" of her life were things that he valued highly. They would leave a permanent mark on his heart and refresh his soul continually. The bottom line was, the Shulammite woman was beautiful to him because everything about her character was good. The "fruits" of her life mirrored the fruit of the Spirit, and she was downright irresistible!

When we walk and live in a way that pleases God, we can't help but attract the appreciation of man. You might feel that the Shulammite's standard of beauty is impossible to attain, but it isn't. You might say, "Well, Michelle, I don't have thick black locks of hair cascading down my back. I don't have lovely olive skin and breasts like fawns. I have short thin brown curls that won't behave to save my soul. I'm flat-chested. I'm overweight."

Whatever, girl—it doesn't matter! In all actuality there are probably only ten women on the face of the earth with absolutely perfect looks, and they paid for that perfection. So just deal with this little reality.

Besides, females tend to major in areas that men minor in. Also, one man's trash is another man's treasure. Beauty is truly in the eye of the beholder. Personally, I think the saying should be: Beauty is in the eye of a man's ego. If you've ever wondered how a good-looking man ends up with a not-so-attractive woman, the answer will always be the same: He likes the way he feels when he is with her. She knows she can't rely on her looks, so her personality and her attentiveness become her greatest assets. She takes the focus off of herself and builds him up, and he loves it! He treats her like a queen because she makes him feel like a king. You see? Even in romance you reap what you sow. A happy man makes a happy woman.

LIFE BEYOND MAYBELLINE

So what's the big beauty secret here? It's not being thin. Don't you feel relieved to know you can stop starving yourself? It's not in having perfect teeth (that's just my hang-up). It's not even about great hair! It's just about your being the best woman you can be, inside and out. Work with what you've got.

When you've achieved your own personal best, you're going to feel good about yourself—not *full of* but *comfortable with* yourself. That's going to change the way you carry yourself. Your different attitude will attract a different type of attention, 'cause when you're comfortable with you, others will be too. They'll want a piece of whatever it is you're smiling about.

I went through a period of my life where I could not face anyone without my makeup on (pun intended). Once you rang my doorbell, you would have to wait outside until I had painted my face and applied mascara in full bloom. It was ridiculous. One night shortly after I got saved I dreamed that God asked me for all of my makeup. Well, I was mortified. How could I confront the world without my mask? Yet, little by little, I began to comply. And I made a revolutionary discovery: People liked the real me. They thought I had a beautiful face without the paint I applied so carefully!

I was free! In a sense I was like Adam and Eve in the days before the Fall: naked and unashamed. I learned that less was more—more attractive to the men around me. They celebrated the natural me. I wondered why no one had told me I was fine just the way I was. But eventually I realized that I had ignored others' hints along that line, so entrenched was I in the way I had always conducted my beauty regime. I hadn't even noticed it wasn't working. Thank God for the Holy Spirit who will lead us into all truth, even beauty secrets, if we let him.

LESSON FROM A QUEEN

When Esther was being prepared as candidate for the king's bride, she went through a serious beauty treatment. It lasted all of twelve months! Now, that is what I call a visit to the spa. The women who were to be presented to the king were soaked in oil of myrrh for six months and then another six months in various perfumes and cosmetic treatments. What a life! If you weren't absolutely ravishing by the time they were finished with you, I guess you could hang it up.

But don't miss the point of this exercise. Women had to undergo these treatments to remove any stench of the life they left behind. It was an act of purification and preparation to meet the standards that brought pleasure to the king. Keep in mind that these women came from all over the province. They had their own customs and products for beauty enhancement—their own line of Maybelline, you might say. But now they were entering a different lifestyle. They were at the palace to please one person—the king. Though they were all virgins and therefore considered pure, nothing of their old life was to remain. It had to be removed, right down to their pores. Yes, even the smell of their skin had to be dealt with. So they were treated with scents that delighted the king.

A note here for all of you who are no longer virgins, who have battled with guilt over your past sexual history or even recent mistakes. I want to take a moment to encourage you. It's time to get over it and move on. This is why Jesus died. He has paid the price for that sin, so stop presenting the bill. Don't you see that blood-colored stamp spelling out the word PAID across your old debt? Too many spend all of their time nursing and rehearsing past mistakes instead of embracing the forgiveness God freely offers. For those who sincerely repent, he extends two things in his hands: forgiveness and the power to be victorious from here on out. Receive both and set yourself free.

My friend, Jesus is able to restore your purity. And when he does, you must learn to do as he does and throw your past mistakes into the sea of forgetfulness. Allow him to be your confidante with unresolved issues that you still battle. Do not "share" these with every man you meet and then wonder why he rejects you. I recommend that you disclose personal mistakes only when you are in a committed relationship and what you've done in the past affects your future as a couple. Be sensitive to the leading of the Lord in this one.

Now, back to the Persian spa. After all of this intense beautification, the day would come when the women were ready to be presented to the king. This was sort of an audition for the role of wife. If he was pleased with you, he would keep you, and if he was not, you were sent to forever abide as just another member of his harem. He might call for you again, and then again, he might not.

Now on this night the candidate for bride was given her choice of attire. All of the other girls proceeded to take whatever they wanted. But Esther was different. Esther asked the eunuch, who had been in the king's employ for quite some time, what he thought she should wear.

Girlfriend, this is something you don't want to miss. The other girls probably picked what to wear based on what they thought had worked for them in the past. But it didn't work for the king. They were all rejected and sent to live in the harem, never to be seen again. All except Esther. Esther did a very wise thing. She sought the advice of someone who knew.

I bet you've been doing what you've been doing for a very long time. Let's all 'fess up. It hasn't worked. If it did work, it worked on the wrong bus. And you got taken somewhere you didn't want to go. So now we're dealing with getting your head together. Hair, head—they're one and the same because at the end of the day, a pretty head of hair with nothing inside is unattractive indeed. A pretty house with no one home makes the bus stop for only a minute unless the bus is empty too. So get your head together by seeking wise counsel and taking the advice rendered. Don't get defensive at constructive criticism; use it to your advantage and get free. Don't be afraid to let go of some old habits and embrace a new line of thought.

Consider well the source you choose to advise you. Esther did. You see, the eunuch had been working for the king for a long time. He knew what the king liked. The eunuch obviously liked Esther and was an advocate, kind of like the Holy Spirit is for us. He was not in competition with Esther, so it didn't cost him anything to give advice that would work to Esther's advantage. And he was successful at what he did. These are the three qualities you must look for in your source of advice: knowledge, objectivity, and success.

That would not add up to another single person with a string of messy relationships behind her. Ask someone who is in a successful, committed relationship. Obviously she did something right to get there. Esther listened to the eunuch. When it came to advice concerning Boaz, Ruth listened to her mother-in-law, Naomi. Both women got their man!

The eunuch told Esther what to wear. The right dress is important. Dressing is more than a physical thing. It reflects your persona, the countenance of your spirit. All that fruit that the king raved about with the Shulammite woman should be evident in your life as the fruit of the Spirit. Ask the Holy Spirit what you should wear daily in terms of attitude as well as what you put on your body. He knows how to dress you for your Boaz. He has information you don't. He knows what your Boaz likes.

Now, girl, don't stand with your hands on your hips and say, "Look, Michelle, I've been teasing my hair to high heaven and spraying it stiff as a board for as long as I can remember. I can't let it down for him to run his fingers through now!" Don't tell me,

"But I've been wearing this black eyeliner around my lips for the last twenty years!" An extensive poll revealed that these are two pet peeves of men: untouchable hair and unkissable lips. If that man likes soft, understated lipstick that looks natural, serve it up, sister: we're going for the finish line here! The bottom line is that we can all stand to improve ourselves. Change should not be viewed as a negative concession, but as a positive adventure.

A note here: Don't think of losing weight, changing your hair, wearing less makeup, or even finding trendier clothes as exercises you must undertake to get a man. Instead, take on each of these challenges as self-improvement steps toward being the best you can be for *you* and for the one who loves you most: the Lord himself. Being in good physical shape pleases him because you are taking care of your temple, his creation. Grooming yourself pleases him because you represent him every time you walk out your door. Therefore you should look as well cared for as a member of a royal family.

STYLIN' AND PROFILIN'

Trust me, God has great taste. He likes only the finest of everything. So if you aim for catching his eye and his pleasure, no man will be able to resist you. The bottom line on beauty? It's hard work because it comes from within. Too many of us paint the outside without dealing with the inside, and it mars the finish every time. God wants the man he places in your life to love you from the top of your head to the tips of your toes, inside and out.

You might say, "Michelle, to be perfectly honest, I feel worse after reading your description of the Shulammite woman because I've been a plain Jane all of my life. Others tell me I look nice, but I just don't feel beautiful at all!"

My dear sister, as long as your focus remains on you and your attributes, you will miss it. The beauty in all of us is not our own.

It is only as we release the beauty of the Lord that we are transformed from ugly ducklings into exquisite creatures that capture the hearts of those who are looking for a safe haven in which to rest.

"From Zion, perfect in beauty, God shines forth" (Psalm 50:2). God is the finisher of our beauty regime. It is he who gives us our flawless finish. Without him we are mere mannequins standing in the window of life. No man wants to touch a mannequin, but a godly woman—that's another story. A man knows that this is a woman he can trust with his heart. And a safe haven for all he holds dear will always be the most beautiful sight of all.

Want the bus to stop and take notice? You better put on the right dress, girl, and keep those arms down!

Dear Heavenly Father, for far too long I have relied on the external and ignored the internal. I have used my body in inappropriate ways to get attention. I have masqueraded as someone I was not. I am weary from the effort of it all.

Inside I have died quietly, longing to be loved for just being me. I have been afraid to release the real me for fear of rejection, and yet you tell me I am fearfully and wonderfully made. Help me to believe that and begin again. Help me to strip away everything that is unnecessary and free me to be who you created me to be. Help me to rejoice in the way you made me and see my value through your eyes.

Remind me daily that when you formed me you said, "It is good." I am good! Lord, I stand in agreement with you now. Tell me how to dress to be pleasing to you. Tell me how to groom myself to please the one you are preparing me for, that he too might see me as a good thing. I want to be crafted by your hand as a vessel beautiful to behold, yet bearing things within that are even more wonderful. Above all, Lord, help me to be a crystal-clear reflection of you, in Jesus' name. Amen.

THREE

BUS STOPS AND YIELD SIGNS

So the LORD God caused the man to fall into a deep sleep.
GENESIS 2:21

And now, a CNN update: Sources have reported that an epidemic is sweeping the single community at an alarming rate. The disease, "One-tree-itis," has odd symptoms that are leaving the most noted experts befuddled. It seems this malady makes you focus on and long for the one thing you can't have. Over time victims of this ailment become paralyzed, dysfunctional, or even worse—they self-destruct.

The FDA (the Flesh and Death Administration) has approved a medication to treat the symptoms of "One-tree-itis: It's called Willful Indulgence. It's no cure, however, and in fact has serious side effects. It seems that each dose, though alleviating feelings of loneliness, eventually leaves the patient in an even deeper state of self-pity, while inspiring obsessive-compulsive behavior, excessive feelings of entitlement, and all-out rebellion, which could lead to death or to the slow torment of dissatisfaction. Many of this disease's victims have reported finding themselves unable to enjoy the fruit even after they have bitten into it.

A physician famous for curing even the "incurable," Jesus of Nazareth, stated that the only antidote for "One-tree-itis" is Absolute Surrender.

I know you don't want to go there, but we must. You see, in order to catch the bus, you've got to wait for it. Waiting is about surrendering to the yield sign. It's about sitting patiently at the bus stop. What happens when you don't master this one thing? You land in a puddle of trouble. The bus goes by at top speed and makes a mess of your dress—I'm a witness.

Let me share a little story with you. During college, shortly before I came to the Lord, I was dating a rock star from Los Angeles. Don't ask me who, 'cause I ain't tellin'. I was madly in love with this man, yet I felt God tugging at my heart, and I gave in. I accepted him as Lord and Savior of my life. This, of course, meant that some very significant things changed in my relationship with this man—some things he didn't appreciate. I could see the glaze coming over his eyes as I tried to explain why I had to live a holy life. He wasn't having it. He said he was a Christian, too, accused me of being judgmental, and off he went.

I was cool with that in the beginning. You see, I had made a deal with God. I told God that I would live holy if he would clean up this man and bring him back to me as my husband in the course of a year. Wasn't that kind of me to give God a whole year?

Well, wouldn't'cha know an entire year came and went, and this man didn't look as if he was thinking about God at all. He moved on to another relationship, but I was steadfast. I was keeping the faith, believing for his salvation and his return—all of this against the advice of every single one of my close friends. I silenced their cautions by saying, "You don't *understand*." After all, I had heard from God, I thought, and he was going to cooperate with my plan. They hoped for my sake that he could pull it off.

A year went by, and another. I moved to Los Angeles; I moved back to Chicago. Then another year. And another. My friends no longer had anything to say when I brought him up; they just got a look on their faces and pressed their lips together.

Meanwhile, everything else about my life was fabulous, though I didn't notice. I was excelling in my advertising career, flying all over the country producing television commercials with the rich, the famous, and the not-so-famous. Yet all of my attention was focused on this one area of my life that continued spiraling downward. I was in bondage to my own desire. I could not let go of this man. Though he tried to be patient with me, while keeping me at arm's length, I'm sure he thought I was absolutely out of my mind. I couldn't even consider the advances of other men around me. I felt guilty, as if I was cheating on him! Was this madness or what?

Finally, four years later (yeah, four *years*), things came to a head. I confronted him and asked if he was ever going to come to his senses and marry me. He said simply that I should forget about him because he was *never* going to get married.

I was devastated, angry, and confused. Had God pulled the wool over my eyes? How could I have been so foolish? I revisited all my rationalizations. I had put out countless fleeces in order for God to confirm that this man was my husband, and I thought I got the answers I wanted. But obviously God had long been silent, leaving me to be my own Holy Spirit.

I didn't want to hear the truth. I didn't want to face the answer, but I finally realized I had to if I was to go any further with God. I had to accept the fact that my own willfulness and deafness to the Holy Spirit and loving counsel had landed me in this distressing heap. After many tears and much prayer, I pulled myself up on the road to recovery and moved on with my life.

HATH GOD SAID?

As I healed, several years came and went. Then it happened. A friend of mine had become quite enamored with a minister she had met. She asked if I would allow him to pray for me. Of course I always welcome prayer, so I allowed him to pray. While in prayer he got the "unction" to tell me that I was going to meet my husband in the next two days. Also that this man was very handsome, very wealthy, and definitely worth the wait I had endured.

The next day I found myself wandering through a store that I hadn't visited since the last time the rock star had come to town. I shook my head as I reflected on all that had transpired between us for so many years and wondered curiously if God would now choose to give him back to me now that I was completely over him. I then dismissed the idea as I pondered the prophecy I had been given.

Wouldn't you know, bright and early the next morning, the telephone rang. This was to be the big day, remember? I answered and it was him—yeah girl, the rock star! I have to tell you, my blood ran cold. I was terrified. This was an unusual occurrence. Though he had dangled carrots in front of me all those years to keep me hanging on with no intention of ever coming back to me, he rarely called. As a matter of fact, it had been two years since I had spoken with him. I tried to remain calm as he greeted me warmly and asked me how I had been doing.

"Fine," I managed to croak. I barely heard it over the beating of my heart.

"Guess what?" he said. "I'm getting married! I know we haven't talked much over the years, but I wanted you to know how special you are to me. I really, really love you, and I wanted you to be among the first I shared my good news with."

Can you imagine? I was angry. I was relieved. I was angry. I was confused. I was angry. I couldn't make up my mind what I felt. Just when I thought I had recovered from losing him, I was thrown into a tailspin. The devil showed up to remind me that I had put years of my life on hold, waiting for this man's return to me. Though I had moved on, this seemed to be too cruel an ending for a very difficult period of my life. I had nothing to show for all I had been through with this man except the pain of rejection, embarrassment, and a million questions for God.

How had I opened the door to be so painfully deceived? After all, I had waited on God, hadn't I? Then the answer came. I had not been waiting on God. I had been waiting on my own desires. Even my submission to his Word had held a selfish agenda. I had used my obedience to God as a bartering tool! I was willing to be a good little spiritual do-right if my goodness would be rewarded with what I wanted.

That was more dangerous than I knew at the time, but I was in too deep. I had sped past every caution and yield sign, driven by my longings. The serpent had convinced me that the fruit of marriage was good to the flesh, pleasing to the self-esteem, desirable for attaining status and validation. Therefore I, like Eve, had taken my life into my own hands. I had chosen a mate according to my own specifications—according to the lust of my flesh and the pride of life. And on that note my heart plummeted out of the Lord's safekeeping, rolled into the world, and settled on the corner of Lonely Place and Self-Will Drive: "For everything in the world—the cravings of sinful man, the lust of his eyes and the boasting of what he has and does—comes not from the Father but from the world" (1 John 2:16).

It was not a very nice neighborhood. All kinds of strange men lived there, and since I hadn't learned my lesson, I kept getting on the wrong bus and finding myself further away from my destination. No one seemed to know where Commitment Boulevard was. If they did, they weren't stopping. Finally I ran out of gas and change. I couldn't even find a rumpled-up transfer! As I came crawling back into the presence of God, dragging all of my "whys" behind me, he answered very gently, though he had two very firm opinions to offer. The first was, "You became a slave to the longing for love." Scripture says, "For a man is a slave to whatever has mastered him" (2 Peter 2:19).

He elaborated, "You allowed your desire for a mate to master you instead of trusting and resting in me." That cut me to the core as I absorbed the truth of it. You know why bondage is such hard labor? Because a slave is never paid. Yet you get sucked into the awful cycle of feeling you must perform for the wage of love, so you do a flip and come up empty-handed. This just promotes jumping higher, dancing faster, and singing louder—but to no avail. In the end you find yourself singing to an empty house. Yet God who loved us first, and is so much more deserving of all our efforts, stands waiting for us to simply turn our affections toward him. Oh, the poetic injustice of it all!

I could relate to Leah in the book of Genesis as she expended all of her energy performing to win Jacob's love. But Jacob didn't love her. He had chosen another. (This is why it is so important to allow that man to choose you.) Jacob loved Rachel, and nothing Leah did could change that.

"Leah became pregnant and gave birth to a son. She named him Reuben, for she said, 'It is because the LORD has seen my misery. Surely my husband will love me now'" (Genesis 29:32). The girl went through this exercise three times before she finally got it. She kept birthin' babies and hoping one would win her favor with her husband, but all it did was win him more time with his beloved Rachel. Finally on the fourth try, she made a different declaration: "She conceived again, and when she gave birth to a son she said, 'This time I will praise the LORD.' So she named him Judah" (Genesis 29:35).

Leah finally got the right idea. She turned her affections toward God and chose to hide her hurting heart in him...for a while, anyway. The sad thing about Leah and myself was that while we were busy concentrating on the one thing we couldn't have, we missed all the blessings that were available. We were like Eve, who failed to take note of all the other trees she could eat from and instead focused on the one she couldn't have. The tree of life was among the "any tree" category that she was permitted to eat from—a much better selection, yes?

What trees had slipped past Leah's vision? Leah didn't comprehend the fruit of her labor or the significance of the children that she bore. As she tussled for Jacob's love, she gave birth to half of the tribes of Israel! If only she had realized the incredible blessings that God had bestowed on her, how great her joy would have been. But she was focused on that one tree.

If only you could see the work that the Lord is doing in you—the rich fruit that your life will bear to bless others in the future—it would be hard to feel dejected. Ironically, Leah's sister Rachel had "One-tree-itis" too. Though she had Jacob's love, she had no children. In her eyes this seriously dampened the joy of being loved. "When Rachel saw that she was not bearing Jacob any children, she became jealous of her sister. So she said to Jacob, 'Give me children, or I'll die!'" (Genesis 30:1).

Have you ever felt that life without a mate was not a desirable proposition? The scary part of this scenario is that Rachel died in childbirth. Sometimes the thing you think you will die without is the very thing that will kill you. Be careful what you ask God for. The serpent keeps us squirming as we attempt to stop performing, stop trying to help God fulfill our wishes, and rest in him. Yet with the firm resolve of a parent who has decided his overtired child needs to take a nap, God allows us to wrestle against sleep until we wear ourselves out. Yes, rest we must.

I have to raise one more point before I move on. Jacob asked Rachel a very interesting question after she demanded a child from him: "Jacob became angry with her and said, 'Am I in the place of God, who has kept you from having children?'" (Genesis 30:2).

Is a man taking God's place in your life? Does having a mate take precedence over all of the other blessings and opportunities you've been given? That is idolatry, sister, and you know how God feels about that. All idols will fall. In this case their falling will usually come in the form of their failing us in some way that brings deep pain to our hearts. Perhaps this is why God told the Israelites in captivity that when they turned to him with undivided hearts and sought him wholeheartedly, *then* they would find him and he would turn their captivity around. As you begin to get rid of the idols in your life and turn your heart to God, you will find a Lover who responds to your simply being you.

Mary, the sister of Martha, had no problem with the concept that she didn't need to perform for love. While Martha slaved in the kitchen, getting madder by the minute at her lack of help, Mary sat at the feet of Jesus, drinking in his every word. She loved Jesus, and he loved her back. But as you know, misery loves company, so Martha tried to get her to perform too. Jesus gently tried to help Martha get a revelation. There was no need for all that work, he told her—there was an easier way and Mary had found it. Jesus said, "Only one thing is needed. Mary has chosen what is better, and it will not be taken away from her" (Luke 10:42).

Mary had chosen to totally submerge herself in her love relationship with the Lord, and that would never be taken from her. She sought God with all of her heart. She held nothing in reserve. All else paled in comparison with Jesus in her eyes. She was totally consumed with him. She was confident that she had his love and attention. Instinctively she knew this was a winning investment. Others had failed her, but Jesus wouldn't.

Isn't that what we're all looking for? A love that won't be taken away from us, a love in which we can rest secure? There is only one Man who provides that type of love: the ultimate Lover of our souls, Jesus himself. In his love alone can we truly rest.

It is only in a state of rest that we are able to make quality decisions. This was where I needed to be, more focused on God than man. On that note I declared a "man fast" to clear my spiritual palate. I had lost my taste for the will of God while feasting on all the wrong fruit.

HOW TO WORK IT OUT

The second thing God said to me was this: "You need to persevere so that when you have done the will of God, you will receive what he has promised" (Hebrews 10:36).

This was a hard saying for me. I had wanted God to give me what I wanted first, and then I would give him what he wanted. So he left me to my own devices. He chose not to argue with me, but allowed me to believe what I wanted until I was ready to listen to him. Little did I understand, he had no intention of robbing me of the desire of my heart. He longed for me to be a totally fulfilled and happy person, but he was the only One who knew the way to bring that into fruition in my life. As long as I did the picking and choosing, as long as I dictated to him what I needed instead of seeking what he had in mind, I would find myself in bondage and deception.

He had a plan for my life, and he has one for yours: plans for good, and not for evil. He has a plan to give you a determined end. He has a happy ending written out for you and for me, but we won't get to read it if we don't let him write it.

TO MARRY OR NOT TO MARRY?

The episode I shared with you at the beginning of this chapter happened more than fifteen years ago. I am still single. Let me ask you a question. What if God told you that you weren't going to get married for ten years? What would you do in the meantime? How would you live your life differently? What would you say if God told you that you were never going to get married?

Ooh! Did a wave of nausea wash over you? Did your stomach involuntarily grip? Did you break out in a cold sweat? It's a hard thing to answer, isn't it? Yet answer it we must. Or we face an even greater question. Consider this thought: "An unmarried woman or virgin is concerned about the Lord's affairs: Her aim is to be devoted to the Lord in both body and spirit. But a married woman is concerned about the affairs of this world—how she can please her husband" (1 Corinthians 7:34).

What are you really concerned about—devoted to "in both body and spirit"? I have to admit I spent a major part of my single existence concerned about everything *except* the Lord's affairs. I was more concerned about my affairs. Why? Because I wasn't in love with the Lord. Are you in love with the Lord, or just giving him lip service?

Okay, I'll be honest first. In my man-idol days, I said I loved the Lord, but I wanted to be in love with someone else—someone I could hold and touch. I was in bondage to the notion of being married, and so I was concerned about the things of this world. I wasn't thinking about pleasing anyone but myself. I was held captive by my own self-centeredness.

Yet I chose to blame my captivity on God. I believed he was withholding happiness from me. And I was like a pouting child determined to hold my breath until he gave me my way. Little did I know how unfazed he would be by this exercise. After I became literally asphyxiated by my desperation, my desire to live motivated me to exhale and get another point of view. Here it is: Your life as a single should not be viewed as confinement to captivity, but as liberation to opportunity—opportunity to live the fullest life imaginable. "How full can life possibly be without a mate?" you ask. You'd be surprised. But let me finish making my case on the importance of living your life on purpose each and every day.

WHAT A DIFFERENCE A DAY MAKES

When the Israelites were led into Babylonian captivity, they refused to believe their dilemma was real. Many a false prophet "prophe-lied" to the people that their stay in Babylon would be a short one. But then the prophet Jeremiah showed up, telling a different story.

> This is what the LORD Almighty, the God of Israel, says to all those I carried into exile from Jerusalem to Babylon: "Build houses and settle down; plant gardens and eat what they produce. Marry and have sons and daughters; find wives for your sons and give your daughters in marriage, so that they too may have sons and daughters. Increase in number there; do not decrease. Also, seek the peace and prosperity of the city to which I have carried you into exile. Pray to the LORD for it, because if it prospers, you too will prosper." Yes, this is what the LORD Almighty, the God of Israel, says: "Do not let the prophets and diviners among you deceive you. Do not listen to the dreams you encourage them to have. They are prophesying lies to you in my name. I have not sent them," declares the LORD.
>
> This is what the LORD says: "When seventy years are completed for Babylon, I will come to you and fulfill my gracious promise to bring you back to this place. For I know the plans I have for you," declares the LORD, "plans to prosper you and not to harm you, plans to give you hope and a future. Then you will call upon me and come

and pray to me, and I will listen to you. You will seek me and find me when you seek me with all your heart. I will be found by you," declares the LORD, "and will bring you back from captivity." (Jeremiah 29:4–14)

Seventy years? "I haven't got seventy years to be single, Michelle!" I hear you! I used to tell God my name wasn't Sarah.

But notice this: *Who* led the Israelites into exile? God himself, because of their refusal to yield to his plan for their lives. That's right—some of us are in self-imposed exile, while some of us God has put on hold, waiting for his plan to unfold. But the truth remains: We cannot sit and count the days going by while we wait for a mate to show up. And if we run after a moving bus, we'll either get left in the dust or run over. Therefore it behooves us to do what God told Adam to do as the first couple was led out of Eden. We must cultivate that from which we have been taken. We must do what the Israelites were instructed to do in Babylonian captivity. Live life to the fullest where you are. Increase, don't decrease. Don't think about tomorrow—God has your tomorrow covered.

In order to live victoriously as singles, we must get to the place where we live *contentedly,* without expecting our circumstances to change. It is in living for today, as the day presents itself, that we become healthy, whole individuals—satisfied women who would be blessings in the lives of men. Remember, it doesn't take two halves to make a couple; it takes two whole people coming together to become a tribute to oneness.

THE WHOLE PIE

How do you become a whole person? By choosing to live each day *in* purpose, *on* purpose. Let me give you some background on the passage we just read in Jeremiah. Why were the Israelites in captivity, anyway? When God handed down the specifics of the Law in the book of Leviticus, one of his mandates was that his people give the land a Sabbath every seven years. Though the Israelites didn't understand why at the time, God had a purpose for this instruction. This was so the earth could rejuvenate itself, restore all of its rich mineral deposits so that it could produce bountiful crops. If the people continually planted without giving the earth a rest, the ground would not be as fertile, and the crops would begin to degenerate in quality. The Lord even anticipated the Israelites' concerns over what would become of them if they missed a year of planting. So he let them know he had them covered: "You may ask, 'What will we eat in the seventh year if we do not plant or harvest our crops?' I will send you such a blessing in the sixth year that the land will yield enough for three years. While you plant during the eighth year, you will eat from the old crop and will continue to eat from it until the harvest of the ninth year comes in" (Leviticus 25:20–22).

Is that deep or what? God was going to make supernatural provision for Israel so the land would have a chance to renew its fruitfulness. He will do the same for us. God will supernaturally meet our needs if we will allow him to. But like the Israelites, when we don't trust him to do that, we take matters into our own hands and end up in bondage. The Israelites were afraid to trust God to fill in the slack so they continued to plant without stopping for 490 years! They never allowed the land to rest.

I wonder if anybody did the arithmetic as he or she was being led away to Babylon. "Let's see. Seven years of refusal to rest divided into 490 years of disobedience equals…well, what do you know? Seventy years of bondage!" This lets us know that when God says, "Give it a rest," he means to have his way.

And the end of the story? "The land enjoyed its sabbath rests; all the time of its desolation it rested, until the seventy years were completed in fulfillment of the word of the LORD spoken by Jeremiah" (2 Chronicles 36:21).

Never mind that God had his reasons for telling them to give the land a break every seven years. Never mind that God has his reasons for your being single right now. You can continue to toil away when he has asked you to rest and find yourself in Babylon.

I remember walking to the bus stop one cold morning many years ago with tears streaming down my face. I asked God why he allowed me to be subjected to so much pain and rejection. He said one profound thing to me that I will never again forget, though I did for a season. He said, "Because I am going to give you a love ministry." The End, by God.

I couldn't wrap my head around that at the time. So I continued my rough ride down love's highway until I finally crashed and burned. I raised my puny fists toward the sky and said, "God, I am so sick and tired of being sick and tired, you've got to do something! I don't want you to give me a mate until you can prove to me that I can be happy with just you. How can I tell anyone that you're enough if I don't believe it myself?"

Sound bold? Well, I always did like to live my life dangerously. But God knew the plans he had for me even when I couldn't see them. He has a plan for you too. You've got to rest in that knowledge. Remember Adam, how peacefully he slept as God fashioned the perfect mate for him? He didn't jump up every five seconds and demand to know how far along God was. No, the Word says that he was in a deep sleep. He rested secure in the purpose of God for his life.

Don't forget that Adam didn't wake up until Eve was finished. So why not rest and allow God to finish what he has begun in you? How do you rest? Obey the yield sign. Settle in at the bus stop. You can't travel and rest at the same time. And don't start telling God which way to take your life, either! Just sit down and take a load off. His burden is lighter than yours.

And stop looking at your watch. Time is nothing more than man's measurement of God's infinite space. God measures the need for movement against the completion of his purposes. What does that mean? Nothing new happens until the first order is completed. So trust me, God wrote the bus route and the schedule so there is no need to map out your journey to the altar. He is well able to get you to the church on time—his perfect time.

Dear Heavenly Father, help! I've fallen and I can't get up. Every time you reach to help me, I struggle against your efforts and hurt myself. I am so wounded it's hard to find a spot where I can rest. I continue to toss and turn in my own will. I struggle to let go of my desires to you. I surrender them for a time, then snatch them back again when I feel you've taken too long to answer.

Forgive me for my impatience and conditional love. Help me to love you the way that you love me—faithfully, with no prerequisites attached. I long to understand the height, the depth, the width of your love for me and celebrate it.

I desire to lose sight of all that is temporal as I give in to your eternal embrace. Be my comfort and the Lover of my soul. Fill me to overflowing with your peace that surely passes all of my understanding.

As I release all that I grip so tightly in my hands, touch and heal the scars my willfulness leaves behind. Tuck me beneath your love and let me rest my head on the pillow of your assurances. And as I sleep, complete the work that you've begun in me, in Jesus' name. Amen.

Who can say when the heart
      makes its decision
            or by whose clock it chooses to sound
                  signaling the quickening
                        of its pulse
                  the rise in temperature
                        the struggle to keep pace
                              with accelerated breaths
                  in a moment it seems
            unexplainable
                  imperceptible
                        it merely
                              disassociates itself from reason
                                    to stake its own claims
                                          to revel in dancing for no chronicled
                                          purpose
                                                just because…
                              oh just because
                                    because it feels better to fly without
                                    thought
      to celebrate a departure from the norm
                  to nestle in a place that strangely feels like home
who knows
      who can say when is the right time to fall in love
                  to release one's self into another's arms
                        to say yes to it all
                  to bravely give yourself away
                        and feel the better for it
            who can say
      who can say when it's right to stand with extended hands
                        open
                              freely giving what you once held dear

who can say…
can it be that no friend can step forward
no enemy can give deceptive warnings
no earthly alarm can say what the pain in my heart says best
what my feet should have known
that once again I had moved too soon
a step out of time
I allowed my heart to clasp the hands of the
wrong partner
and dance to the wrong rhythm
at the wrong party
on the wrong night
at the wrong time…

PART TWO

THE RIGHT TIME

FOUR

TRIPPIN' OR TRAVELIN'

So the LORD God banished him from the Garden of Eden
to work the ground from which he had been taken.

GENESIS 3:23

Adam and Eve were booted out of the Garden as punishment, but also as a protective measure to save them from living eternally in sin. Sometimes as singles we feel booted out, locked out of that privileged garden called marriage that looks like Eden to us. The moment we, like Adam and Eve, choose to turn our hearts away from God and toward a man to be our source of happiness and fulfillment, we too feel their sense of separation from the kingdom. We feel cast off and left to wander on our own, pondering the meaning of life, love, and the pursuit of happiness.

This is our lot in life, we conclude—to exist as second-class citizens, the oddballs of society, enduring sideward glances as people whisper amongst themselves about our unfortunate state of affairs. After all, something must be wrong with us because we are…alone. They scratch their heads. There must be some hidden fault. After all, we look perfectly normal on the outside. We seem to be sane enough. So what could be the problem?

So how do we cope with not being in the Garden, that perfect place of rest and tranquility? How do we wait for our bus with determination, not despair? How do we avoid trippin' over travelin'? The fact is, we don't need other people's glances and spoken or unspoken criticism to remind us about our "strange" single fate. We are always acutely aware of what is missing. No matter what else God is doing in your life, this little voice in the back of your head keeps whining, "Well, this is fine, but what about *that?* When is he gonna give you *that?*" Yup—shades of One-tree-itis at work. Listening to that little voice will get you in a lot of trouble.

I remember that voice. I met it years ago as a new believer. The woman who had been my spiritual mentor called to tell me that she was getting married. I knew her testimony—how she had waited on the Lord to bring the right person into her life for seven whole years! I congratulated her on her engagement, then commented with wonder at the fact that she had endured those many years of celibacy before getting married. She answered, "Well, the Lord might make you wait seven years too."

I quickly replied, "Oh, no, he won't! 'Cause if he does I'll backslide!" Little did I know, I hadn't handed my life over yet. I was still watching God out of the corner of my eye to see if he was going to do things my way. This was during the period that I was still bartering: obedience for a man. I had already informed God that he had a year to give me a husband, and after that I wouldn't be responsible for anything that I did. Be celibate for seven years? That was entirely out of the question.

Sometimes I think God has such a great sense of humor. Here I am, twenty years later…need I say more?

I DID IT MY WAY

Actually I do need to say more. You see, as ridiculous as it sounds, I was serious about this. I felt that if I was a good little girl and did everything I was supposed to do, God should reward me with what I wanted. That was the deal. My obedience was entirely intellectual. It had nothing to do with loving God, with wanting to please him, glorify him. I fasted and prayed regularly, avoided temptation, witnessed to unbelievers, and regularly attended church, all to store up brownie points to be applied toward the thing I wanted from God.

I thought this was a reasonable arrangement; after all, my list was very short: a mate. So after seven years the enemy of my soul slithered up to me and said, "Time's up!"

I was shocked. God had not kept his end of the deal! In hindsight I can picture God saying, "What deal? You made a deal—I didn't." But I wasn't hearing any of that at the time. I just decided that God could not be trusted. If I sat around waiting for him to give me a mate, I'd never get one. On that note, I opted to backslide—or, as a dear friend of mine says, "back-tumble," which is closer to the truth. I did this for all of one of the lousiest months of my life.

Whoever said sin was fun left out an important part of the sentence: *for a season*. Try a couple of hours. There is nothing worse than feeling as if your prayers are bouncing off the ceiling and going *splat* on the floor. In those miserable days, God didn't have to be angry at me because I was angry at me enough for both of us. So he just relaxed and waited for condemnation to get the best of me. Did he ever lower the boom? No. He just let me get my feelings hurt. Another round of rejection is always a great way to discover who really loves you. Back to God I crawled. He bandaged my wounds and suggested I get some rest. At this point I had no argument.

Why do we all have so much trouble resting in God? I'll tell you why. Because we're all a bunch of control freaks, that's why. We've gotten so used to handling every area of our lives, we completely freak out when someone suggests that we simply "trust the Lord."

"Trust the Lord?" we shout back. "What do you mean, 'trust the Lord'? Don't you know if I don't do things myself, they'll never get done?"

When I was in high school band, we used to do this exercise called marking time. It was actually marching in place. You didn't move forward or backward, you simply marched in place until you were given the signal to move forward. When the whistle was blown, everyone would then be on the same foot, in the same rhythm, warmed up and ready to move out. I've come to see resting as a sort of marking time. God's prescription for rest is not about lying down and dying, or wasting away pitifully. It is about ceasing from your labors. It is God's gracious call to stop striving, pushing, straining, overexerting yourself in an area of your life that God never called you to take into your own hands.

We are afraid of resting because we view it as abdicating responsibility, but it isn't. Resting does not mean that you are inactive or paralyzed. It means that you take care of the business that is set before you and leave the mate stuff to God. Resting means you trust him to handle what you can't and shouldn't. In the meantime he gives you permission to run after two things: him and your purpose.

Scripture tells us:

Delight yourself in the LORD and he will give you the desires of your heart. (Psalm 37:4)

But seek first his kingdom and his righteousness, and all these things will be given to you as well. (Matthew 6:33)

Ooh! I used to hate those Scriptures! When I heard them, I used to cringe as if someone were scraping her nails across a chalkboard. I did not like those verses because I was too lazy to do the work they implied. When I read them I thought, *You mean actually joyfully pursue God when I am feeling so miserable?* Shoot, it was easier to be depressed. Or so I thought. *You mean turn my focus off of what I want and actively run after righteousness, peace, and joy in the Holy Ghost?*

I tried to reason it out. If I did that, could I really trust God to give me the desires of my heart? What if my desires changed? What if God tricked me into dropping my personal goals, and I never achieved or received them? Somewhere in the back of my mind I had decided God was selfish, so it only made sense that he would trick me into being happy alone and then tell me that now that I was happy, why should he mess it up by giving me a man? Call me crazy, but this is what I thought. So being the gentleman that he is, he just waited…and waited…and waited for me to come to the end of myself.

HANDING IT OVER

Finally my exhaustion got the best of me. I was tired of being depressed. I was bored with myself. I didn't realize being unhappy took so much energy. I figured I might as well apply that energy to being joyful. At least I would have more fun. And while I was at it I could find something to do with myself because my pout-fest hadn't provoked God to hurry up and give me what I wanted. He just didn't seem too impressed with my misery. I decided Paul had the right idea: "Not that I have already obtained all this, or have already been made perfect, but I press on to take hold of that for which Christ Jesus took hold of me" (Philippians 3:12).

God had a purpose for my life. Can you guess what it is? God has a purpose for your life too. Please don't find out the way I did. I had to literally get hit by a truck to get my vision straight. Really! And then it took me a year and a half to recuperate and learn to walk again.

Meanwhile God reminded me of a little project I had started four years before and never finished—a book for singles, called *What to Do Until Love Finds You*. Well, I had nothing else to do as I sat in bed. I refused to get hooked on soap operas, so I wrote to pass the time. Seven books later, the rest is history. Now I am completely consumed in running after my purpose instead of a mate. I am delighting myself in the Lord. I am seeking the kingdom of God first. I'm doing all the things I said that I would never do—and I'm having the time of my life!

Jesus snatched me out of the life I once led to deposit me in the life I now lead. He dangled the promise of a better life in front of me until my misery made me reach for it. He holds the same carrot out to you: a life filled with joy and meaning—not down the road when you've found a man, but right where you are, today. He has a purpose for your life, for your singleness. You are created to affect somebody in your world, no matter where that world is. If you're lost in yourself, you're affecting people the wrong way. It is time to rise up and choose to live joyfully, live everyday on purpose, and rejoice in that purpose.

How do I know God has a purpose for your life? Because he said so!

For those God foreknew he also predestined to be conformed to the likeness of his Son. (Romans 8:29)

I praise you because I am fearfully and wonderfully made; your works are wonderful, I know that full well. (Psalm 139:14)

Before I formed you in the womb I knew you, before you were born I set you apart. (Jeremiah 1:5)

He says the same thing to us that he said to Jeremiah. How was it possible for him to know you before you existed? Simple: Before you existed, his purposes were already set in place. Have you ever decided you wanted to get a new couch for your living room? You had the spot cleared out. You knew about the size and the color you wanted, though you hadn't seen the actual model yet. As you made your rounds from store to store, nothing seemed to suit your fancy. Then, all of a sudden, you turned the corner, and there it was in the window! That was the couch! It was perfect for your purposes. You recognized it right away because that couch was in your mind long before you saw it.

In the same way, you were in the mind of God long before you landed here. He had something in mind, and you became the clothes around his idea, the facilitator of his plan! In his foreknowledge, he was positive you would have just the right disposition for the job at hand. He is so anxious for you to get on with it!

HANDMAIDEN OR UP FOR GRABS

Sometimes I sense God's hurt and dismay that we don't love him enough to be content with his love and promises. I liken it to the question Elkanah asked his wife Hannah in the book of 1 Samuel: "Elkanah her husband would say to her, 'Hannah, why are you weeping? Why don't you eat? Why are you downhearted? Don't I mean more to you than ten sons?'" (1 Samuel 1:8).

Poor Hannah. Though she had the love of her husband, like Rachel, she longed to have a child. Elkanah's other wife, Peninnah, had several children and teased Hannah to provoke her into despair.

Does this sound familiar? Though we have the love of the Lord, we see that other women in his kingdom have what we want—a mate. And that slimy ol' serpent loves to use their situations to irritate and provoke us to envy and misery. Elkanah's question to Hannah is directly in line with the cry of God's heart to us.

"Don't I mean more to you than ten men? five men? one man?"

This story is a good example of how to rest constructively while waiting on God. Every year Elkanah took his entire family up to Shiloh to worship the Lord. When the day came to worship, he gave Peninnah and her children portions to sacrifice, but he always gave Hannah a double portion because he loved her.

This is so true of single women today. God loves you so much! Yes, he has blessed many women with husbands, but to you, the husbandless, he gives a double portion. Think about it. You have a double portion of money because it is all yours. You have a double portion of time, again, all yours. Space? All yours. Possessions? All yours! You don't have to share anything with anybody!

"Well, but I'd like to," you say. Uh-huh, that's what you say now. I remember the day that God told me I would be happier as a single, and I was shocked and appalled. How could he say such a thing when he knew how much I longed for a mate? He assured me my life was easier now because I had to answer to no mere mortal. God the King was in charge! Though I could pretend not to hear God's instruction when I wanted to, I couldn't ignore the physical presence of a husband. On top of it all, God truly indulged me more than any man on earth would. This was true, I realized, and I knew I couldn't argue with him.

In spite of this knowledge, the enemy of your soul makes sure someone is available to upset you about your single state. You, like Hannah, become downhearted and stop eating—stop eating life and all the tasty treats it has to offer. You refuse to discover anything new beyond the walls of your home, your job, and your church. Tears become your food.

Wait a minute! Find something to get involved in, whether it be an art class, theater, or some sort of charity organization. A new hobby opens the door to endless possibilities and relationships to make you excited about life. This isn't an invitation to go "on the prowl" for men in these places—this is just an exhortation to get out of the house! Don't be a spiritual sourpuss. Make sure you do things that promote a healthy love for Jesus, a joyful relationship with him, as you get out there and discover some of the other things he has created.

A LESSON FROM HANNAH

We can learn from Hannah. There she was, unable to appreciate how much her husband adored her because she had, you know, "One-tree-itis." It was a severe case—we can see this because she stopped eating. I'm sorry—nothing makes me stop eating! But then Hannah decided to do something about her situation: She prayed.

I hear you: "But, Michelle, I have prayed and prayed about this mate thing. I'm sick of praying. God is probably sick of my praying. Why bother to bring it up again?"

Wait one minute. Back up. I'm talking about prayer on a whole different level. The Bible says that Hannah was weeping and praying so hard her lips were moving, but no sound was coming out. The priest at the temple thought she was drunk. I imagine she was not a pretty sight, but didn't care: She meant business with God. She told the priest that she was a woman "deeply troubled" and that she had been pouring out her heart to the Lord.

Now, pouring out your heart does not sound like this: "Lord, please give me a husband. Could you make him tall, dark, and handsome? I want him to love me like Christ loved the church: to be kind, sensitive, have a sense of humor, and love to travel...." No! Pouring out your heart is when you get real with God—when you hit the deck in your room and you don't come out until something in your spirit is settled. It is praying until you are speechless. You've cried off all your makeup, your hair is disheveled, and you've emptied out every corner of your soul on the subject, including your disappointment or perhaps even anger at God. Get it all out, but make sure you stay until he gives you an answer. Trust me, he's got a whole lot to say on the subject.

> Give ear and come to me; hear me, that your soul may live. I will make an everlasting covenant with you, my faithful love promised to David. (Isaiah 55:3)

> Therefore I am now going to allure her; I will lead her into the desert and speak tenderly to her. (Hosea 2:14)

Psst! Did you know God wants to talk to you? He'll actually lead you to the desert, that dry place in your soul where no relief exists, to get your attention. Have you let him take you there?

In my case, I had always told God what I wanted. I had never asked him what he wanted from me—or what he wanted to give me. After I had worn myself out completely and collapsed in a very unglamorous heap from all my bad choices, I finally squeaked, "So what did you have in mind?"

Let me tell you, he had a lot in mind. "Give me a year of your life. Don't even think about a man or the desire for one. I want to lay the foundation for the rest of your life, but I need your full attention in order to do it." 'Nuff said. For some reason that released me. It seemed when I had some sort of qualifier from him I was able to relax. I then knew not to even think about a man for at least a year! I could deal with that.

I could live with the knowledge that God was doing *something* with my life. He wanted to make a covenant with me. He would be a faithful Lover. What more did I need? As I released that year of my life to him, he filled my world with unending blessings that brought a greater fulfillment to me than I had ever known. Now *I'm* the one telling *him* that I need another uninterrupted year to complete what is before me! I *never* thought I would hear myself telling God to hold off on bringing me a husband.

Check That Motive

Let's go back to Hannah. Eli the priest blessed her and told her to go in peace. After Hannah received this word from Eli, she went her way, and the first thing she did was eat. Suddenly her face was no longer downcast. The next day she went with her husband to worship the Lord, and then they all went home.

Well, wouldn't you know, shortly after this Hannah became pregnant? Now, before you start telling me that you wish it were that simple, I have to point out something significant: There was something else special about Hannah's prayer besides its honesty. Hannah completely committed her desire to the Lord. Though she wanted a son, she told God that if he gave her one, she would give him back to the Lord. What happened there? Hannah got her desire lined up with the purposes of God.

Let me ask you something. Do you want a husband just for your own pleasure, or do you want a husband because you think being married will help you serve God more effectively? Is this desire about your *own* purposes or the purposes of God? I'm just asking!

Hannah had that baby, and after he was weaned, she delivered him to the temple as promised. Every year she visited her son and took him provisions. That little boy grew up to be one of the greatest prophets in Israel. In the meantime the Lord honored Hannah's sacrifice and her continuous sowing into the kingdom by giving her three more sons and two daughters.

Girl, there is no sacrifice you can make that God won't honor in ways that surpass your expectations. And that is what I call constructive waiting, marking time, resting: lining up your desire with God's purposes and completely committing that desire to God.

The choice is up to you. At the end of the day you will rest, either by choice or by force. So open your hands and let him remove whatever is standing between you and a fulfilled life right now.

EGYPT AND BOOT CAMP

You should be excited about resting! Someone else has to do all the work! You have only to let rest prepare you for the next step. In music the rest is a moment of recovery for the singer or musician to gather strength to move on and execute the next section of the song. No matter what you're going through right now, trust me, you're in training. God is fine-tuning you for your purpose.

Believe me, he's able to use the good, the bad, and the ugly in your life. All the pain I suffered in past relationships gave birth to my organization, HeartWing Ministries.

We've already looked at Hannah. Joseph was another biblical person who had a lot of reasons to be unhappy. You remember Joseph in the book of Genesis—the one with the coat of many colors? Though he had a dream of better days, he woke up to a nightmare when his brothers sold him into slavery. Yet he decided to make the most of his time. He had a sense of purpose. He chose to live every day on purpose.

Are you redeeming your time as a single purposefully? Joseph was truly entitled to have a down-and-dirty pity party for himself. He could have sat around moaning, "Oh, I've seen better days. I used to be my daddy's favorite. I had a pretty coat and everything." But instead, something rose up in him, and I think he said to himself, "All right. If I'm going to be a slave, I'm going to be the best slave there is."

Take a clue from our brother, Joseph, and learn to serve others on purpose. Decide to excel where you are, no matter how much you hate your circumstances. Girl, this is the secret to promotion.

Because of Joseph's attitude God blessed and promoted him. His master decided he was the best thing next to sliced bread. So, incidentally, did his master's wife. But Joseph didn't fall for that. He had his sights on a higher call. He wasn't going to do anything that would endanger his reaching his destination. He resisted her attempts at seduction and chose to be holy on purpose.

Joseph could have easily fallen into blaming God for his circumstances or even feeling entitled to indulge himself to assuage his misery. Instead he stuck to his guns. Some of us get tired and slip from time to time, but Joseph was not the average brother—he refused to offend God and give in to his boss's wife's sinful invitation. Even after being falsely accused of rape by this vindictive woman, Joseph chose to maintain a good attitude on purpose, even as he was thrown into jail.

Some of us would have been tempted to complain long and loud that there is no reward in living holy, but Joseph, he adapted to his situation. Again he was promoted, this time to a supervisor in the jail. Talk about cream rising to the top! In spite of his dark surroundings, Joseph chose to stay in the Spirit on purpose. This put him in position to run into a certain baker and wine steward who would change his life forever, though he didn't know it at the time. (Remember—you never know who's watching you.)

Joseph interpreted dreams for them that came true, but they went their separate ways and forgot all about him. Take another lesson from Joseph! Do you feel a little forgotten, like God has you in some sort of invisible box? Has no one noticed all those fabulous gifts of yours? Not to worry, time will tell.

Suddenly, the pharaoh had a dream that unsettled him, and no one could explain it. The wine steward remembered that some man named Joseph down at the prison was good at dream interpretation, and the next thing you know, Joseph was taken from the prison to the palace. Faster than he could figure out what was going on, he was deposited in front of Pharaoh to spell out his dream. Before he could even say, "Thank God for some fresh air," he was promoted to Pharaoh's right-hand man and even given a wife!

Well, I say! From there Joseph went on to be reconciled to his brothers. Even though he was then in the place of power to get retribution for their wrongdoing toward him, he chose on purpose to forgive those who had abused him.

I suggest you do this too. It's the quickest way out of bondage that I know. The sooner you are able to bless your enemies, those men who hurt you, and release them, the sooner you will be in position to receive a blessing yourself. Unforgiveness, unfortunately, causes us to say negative things—curses, spiritually speaking—about the ones who have offended us. This is dangerous. If we choose to curse others, the Word of God tells us those curses will come upon us and wrap themselves around us like a garment (Psalm 109:18). Ugh! I don't think anyone I've ever been angry at is worth all that trouble. How about you? Release them and get on with the business of living. Bless them and receive a blessing.

This is what Joseph did, and he was restored to his father. Through this reconciliation Joseph saved his nation from starvation and went down in history as one of the stellar examples in the Bible. What an inspiring finish! This was all because he chose to live each day on purpose in spite of his circumstances.

Notice something else: As Joseph learned to serve, he learned the minds and the attitudes of the common class. This would help him when he became a leader. As he was promoted, he acquired administrative and accounting skills that would assist him in running Egypt later. Look at God's wisdom!

What are you being trained for? Don't know? Don't worry! God has his reasons and timing for everything. Remember, he gave Joseph a dream when he was young to show him his future, and

Joseph blabbed it and upset his brothers. Sometimes a plan revealed too soon can cause trouble.

And there is something else we must take into careful consideration. If Joseph had never gone to the prison, he wouldn't have ended up in the palace.

THE WAY TO THE PALACE

You may feel as if you're in the prison right now, hidden from the eyes of men and forgotten by God. But you are only one step away from the palace. God is the only One who can release us from our bondage, the prison of aloneness, and transport us into kingdom living—a life rich with fulfillment. Though the way seems hard, it is the only way for you to get to the palace. You've got to cultivate your purpose right where you are. It is part of the process. You are being groomed for a promotion.

Joseph later named his sons in remembrance of his deliverance. Manasseh meant "God has caused me to forget all of my toil," and Ephraim meant "God has caused me to be fruitful in the land of my affliction." As you embrace your prison, you too will bring forth a Manasseh and an Ephraim.

Are you bearing fruit, girlfriend? Or are you just a shriveled-up prune, constantly complaining over your lot in life? C'mon—don't get bitter, get better! You're not even going to remember any of this in a minute. God promises to wipe all your tears from your eyes and invites you to enter into his joy when you can't find your own.

"But how, Michelle?" you ask. "How do you get into your purpose when you don't know what your purpose is?" Girl, locate your gift. Your gift is the thing you do that others praise—the thing you take for granted because it comes so easily to you. Begin by using your God-given gifts to bless others around you. Then watch those blessings double back to you.

I believe that when we finally do what we were created to do, we discover true joy, fulfillment, and prosperity. Why? Because whatever you love doing, you do well, and people are always willing to pay for a job well done. It is scary to think of the number of people who go to work every day thoroughly hating their jobs. This is not God's plan for your life. As you redirect your goals to coincide with your natural talents, you will be amazed to find the desires of your heart being answered.

A CHANGE OF SCENERY

This is what Ruth did. (Yup, we just switched to another Bible character.) Ruth utilized her natural talents for homemaking to comfort her mother-in-law, Naomi. This was her purpose. This was a joy for her. Suddenly single after the death of her husband, Ruth found herself with no immediate prospects for another marriage. She had married a foreigner who had visited her land in Moab, so she was on home turf when her husband died. But Ruth chose to let go of the familiar on purpose and leave her home to accompany Naomi back to Naomi's native land.

Some of you need a change of scenery from your present environment and usual habits. You need to do something you've never done, visit some places you've never seen. You've been standing on the wrong street, waiting for the bus to arrive. Take the plunge now, while you have the freedom. However, be motivated by the purposes of God. Ruth was motivated by a sincere love for her mother-in-law. She was determined to go and care for her. Ruth chose to love on purpose those who were available to be loved.

This is the answer for those of you struggling with your biological clock. I have proclaimed to the world that mine is no longer ticking—it is broken. I now invest all of my motherly instincts in the life of my niece, Lauren, who fills my heart with unspeakable joy. Before that I was the guardian of two of my nieces from Africa who were attending school in the States.

If your alarm clock is getting ready to go off, reach out to mentor someone's child. He or she will love you for it. And let me tell you, when you care for a child, you are reminded of how much work is involved in being a good parent. That will probably slow down the ticking inside your heart big-time.

Or perhaps children aren't your thing. You just want to be loved. Invest yourself into the lives of your family and friends. Invest yourself in a ministry that touches the needy and the hurting. Begin to reach beyond where you are, pour yourself out on purpose, and watch God fill you up.

Ruth poured herself out in service to Naomi, gleaning in the fields to provide for them both. She worked on purpose. And while she was working, a certain man was watching. Get my drift? That man proceeded to ask questions about her identity. Unbeknownst to her, Ruth had acquired quite a reputation for herself, one of kindness and integrity. This man, Boaz, made special provision for her needs to be met, and Ruth quietly accepted his gestures with grateful humility, staying in her place.

Now, Naomi hadn't gotten old by being a fool. She imparted advice to Ruth, and in the end, Ruth got her man! How? By following Naomi's wise counsel on purpose. In a foreign land, Ruth knew different principles were at work. When she left Moab, she left her own devices behind as well. She lived her life on purpose with an open heart and open hands. She chose to leave behind the idols of her own culture to embrace and serve a God she had not known—on purpose. She was willing and ready to receive whatever God wanted to give. She had no list of requirements. She focused herself totally on giving, trusting that God would provide what was best for her, and in the end she reaped bountifully: a wealthy, loving husband.

Open your hands, my sister; you are now in a different land as well. When you accepted Christ, you left Moab, the old familiar world, and stepped into God's country. You are now a princess in his royal kingdom. The devices of the world don't work well here. They are not befitting a lady of royal stature.

Notice that in both of their cases, Joseph and Ruth had to be removed from where they were to be put into position to receive their mates. This is not always a physical move. It can be spiritual and emotional. Whatever it is in your case, it's time to make that move! So put aside all of your old habits on purpose and get ready for a whole new way of doing things. Stop trippin' and don't travel till God gives you a green light. That is, if you want to get on that bus that's heading your way.

Dear Heavenly Father, I confess that I have put my life on hold. I have not redeemed my single time in a fruitful manner. I have not rested in your plan for my life. Even when I determine to do so, I find myself sneaking peeks over your shoulder to see if I can spy out my desires on the horizon of my life.

I have chosen my own partners, made my own schedule, and insisted on my own way. I have not been concerned with the things that concern you. I have been concerned only with myself.

I struggle with how to get past myself and the needs for companionship that seem to overwhelm me at times. Help me, O God, to turn my eyes toward you and keep them there. Establish my heart in total trust in you. Help me to live each day in the center of your divine purpose, on purpose. Help me to rejoice in the reason you made me and bask in the fulfillment of completing my call.

Fill me up with your love for me. Make it so real that I feel your embrace. Let every empty place in my heart be saturated with the knowing of your care. Let your love be my greatest joy, my greatest strength, my song of songs, in Jesus' name. Amen.

FIVE

TOKENS, TRANSFERS, AND PASSES, OH MY!

They set up kings without my consent;
they choose princes without my approval.

HOSEA 8:4

A t this point you may be asking, "When are we going to get to the juicy part? When are we going to get to the nuts and bolts of how to get this man—I mean, catch this bus?" I hear you! And believe me, we will get to all of that, but I hope by now you understand that in order to accomplish it, a whole lot of groundwork has to be laid. That is, if you want God's best for your life. That is, if you want to live a fulfilled life after you catch the bus.

Some buses have taken me to disappointing destinations. Because I wasn't really sure where I wanted to go, I spent my token without knowing when it was time to get off and rode too long, if you know what I mean. Other times I failed to use my transfer to get on a better bus. And let's not talk about the times when I was coolly informed that we had reached the end of the line. I had to get off and found myself stranded without a pass or a plan.

Can I get a witness? I don't know about you, but as I wrote in a song once, "I've won some wicked hearts and paid the cost"—because I did the choosing. And I made those choices for all of the wrong reasons.

Someone once asked me, "Do you believe there is only one perfect mate for you?" My answer is this. You can live with a lot of people—but excel, walk in the center of God's will for your life? You can't do that with just anyone. I believe the key to living the best life you can, for yourself and for God, lies in being partnered with the right person. Only God knows who that person is. He has chosen that person based on your life purpose. He didn't choose that person based on chemistry or good looks, not that he isn't concerned about those things as well. But he is *more* interested in our being effective and fruitful in our lives.

Remember, God does everything on purpose, including creating you and selecting your mate. Man was made first, to worship God, and second, to supervise the smooth operation of God's creation. When God decided to create a mate for Adam, he said he was designing a mate who was "suitable" for him. That meant she was specially crafted and designed to be everything Adam needed in order to live the way God wanted Adam to live. Woman was made to assist man in completing his God-ordained assignment, to partner with him and equip him to be the best worshiper and supervisor he could be. And vice versa. Fulfilling God's purpose is what everything in our lives is about.

This is why I am pounding this purpose concept into the ground. If you don't know your purpose, you won't recognize the right partner. You've got to get your head together—and I'm not talking about weaves and extensions—or you won't know the right bus when you see it. Why? Because you won't know where you're supposed to be going. As a matter of fact, you won't even know where you're supposed to stand.

As you know, there are designated bus stops. If you stand in the middle of the block where there is no bus stop, you can wave all day, but the bus won't stop. But when you stand in the right place, you won't even have to wave. Catching the bus will be effortless. The bus will automatically stop, because it is under the authority of the One who mapped out its route. Are you getting my drift here?

"Do not conform any longer to the pattern of this world, but be transformed by the renewing of your mind. Then you will be able to test and approve what God's will is—his good, pleasing and perfect will" (Romans 12:2). You cannot select a mate the way the world does. Your selection process has to be different because your purpose for marriage is different. You can make a decent choice on your own, or a good, pleasing, *and* perfect choice based on what God has in mind for your entire life.

Girl, we get so distracted by the bedroom and the qualities that look good in there. Trust me, you will spend most of your life outside that room. But we get distracted by the flesh, totally ignore the Spirit, and get in trouble. A year into a marriage that on the surface looks like a happy one, many have turned to their mates and said these famous words: "You're not making me happy." If he or she wasn't God's choice, then of course not, you nut! That person was not designed for that purpose.

Then the awful truth begins to sink in. The hole in your heart is not a person-sized hole. God should already have filled that one up. That gaping void is a *purpose*-sized hole. Fulfilling your God-ordained purpose is what fulfills an empty soul. The mate is the icing on top.

This is why Satan tries to come along to discourage, irritate, and provoke you. He wants to make you anxious and encourage you to make foolish choices. He knows the wrong mate can mess you up and destroy your entire life design.

ONLY THE STRONG SURVIVE?

The life of Samson provides a stellar example of this. He is the perfect picture of what *not* to do. Before we tackle his story, let me ask you this question: What comes to mind when I say the name *Samson?* Delilah, right? Human nature tends to remember the negative first. Yet there was a whole lot more to the life of Samson that is worthy of our attention. The first thing we need to take note of is the fact that God had a purpose for Samson's life.

> A certain man of Zorah, named Manoah, from the clan of the Danites, had a wife who was sterile and remained childless. The angel of the LORD appeared to her and said, "You are sterile and childless, but you are going to conceive and have a son. Now see to it that you drink no wine or other fermented drink and that you do not eat anything unclean, because you will conceive and give birth to a son. No razor may be used on his head, because the boy is to be a Nazirite, set apart to God from birth, and he will begin the deliverance of Israel from the hands of the Philistines."
>
> The woman gave birth to a boy and named him Samson. He grew and the LORD blessed him, and the Spirit of the LORD began to stir him while he was in Mahaneh Dan, between Zorah and Eshtaol. (Judges 13:2–5, 24–25)

Funny how no one remembers Samson in association with the Spirit of the Lord—how he blessed him and moved in his life. Why not? Because Samson got hooked up with the wrong person. That wrong person rearranged his legacy.

Now for the next question. Did you know that Samson was married? Mmm-hmm, Samson got around, girl: "Samson went down to Timnah and saw there a young Philistine woman. When he returned, he said to his father and mother, 'I have seen a Philistine woman in Timnah; now get her for me as my wife'" (Judges 14:1–2).

"Samson went *down* to Timnah." That's interesting in and of itself. Anytime you see somebody "going down" in Scripture, you know that something is up. God doesn't waste words. The account never states Samson's business in Timnah, but something significant happened while he was there. He saw a Philistine woman and decided he wanted to marry her. This was a young lady who wasn't of the godly persuasion. Why would a Nazirite priest wish to be connected to an idol worshiper? an enemy of God? an unregenerated person? How was this woman going to help him with his ministry?

Your ministry may not be in the church, but you still have one—right where you are working and living every day. For someone, your life is the only Bible they will ever read. So watch where you're walking. The wrong mate can ruin your witness.

Here we have Samson hanging out in the wrong place, mingling intimately with the wrong people. Are you going to the wrong places for the wrong reasons, considering the wrong people for potential mates? You know, people who have no interest in God? Remember that choosing to be friends with the world makes you an enemy to God (James 4:4). You cannot love the world and love God too. God and the world have opposing values—opposing purposes. As you cling to the world, your view and preferences will shift from godly to glandular. Your flesh will become your master. You will begin to resist the call of God's Spirit.

Look at Samson. He saw this girl and forgot his calling. He was supposed to be set apart for God, and there he was hanging out with those beneath his station. He forgot, but his parents didn't.

His father and mother replied, "Isn't there an acceptable woman among your relatives or among all our people?

Must you go to the uncircumcised Philistines to get a wife?"

But Samson said to his father, "Get her for me. She's the right one for me." (His parents did not know that this was from the LORD, who was seeking an occasion to confront the Philistines; for at that time they were ruling over Israel.) (Judges 14:3–4)

We-ell! Isn't that interesting! Actually, many things here are interesting, so we'll take them one at a time. First, Samson's parents wave the caution flag. They nicely remind Samson that he is supposed to marry from among his own people. Likewise, you and I are not to be unequally yoked. We are not to seek out intimate and abiding relationships with unbelievers. "Can two people walk together without agreeing on the direction?" (Amos 3:3, NLT).

It is a well-known fact that the largest sources of contention between married couples are politics, sex, money, and God. Therefore it behooves us to find as much common ground as we can. The foremost area of importance is our potential mate's relationship with God. If that man won't break God's heart, girl, he won't break yours. Got it? It is not good enough that he used to go to church, knows Jesus' cousin, or is "spiritual." "Spiritual" does not necessarily mean "born again." Everyone is spiritual these days. *Is he saved?* Is his heart sold out to God, lock, stock, and barrel? By the way, if you have to explain to him why you can't have sex with him before the two of you get married, he is not "saved" enough! Is he walking the walk, or just talking the talk? He needs to be doing both.

MAMA SAID THERE'D BE DAYS LIKE THIS

It's important to notice that Samson's parents objected to his choice. Why? Because we are dealing with a spiritual dynamic here. Samson's mother and father knew that the Law of God forbade them to intermarry with the heathen. They recognized how crucial Samson's choice would be because of the call on his life. If he had forgotten, they were not going to be shy about reminding him.

Also, the Bible tells us to honor our father and mother so that things may go well with us and we might have a long life (Deuteronomy 5:16). If instead we choose to give them grief and disrespect their instruction, things won't go well with us, and our lives will be shortened because of foolish choices.

In every disastrous marriage relationship I have witnessed, I have posed this question: "What did your parents think of the person you married?" Consistently the answer has been, "Oh, they didn't want me to marry him" or "They did not like her." No matter how old you are, the bottom line on this whole parent thing is this: Your parents are your covering until you get married. God gives them special insight to guide you toward your destiny. This might not always be to your liking, but it is always for your good. This is true no matter what you think of them, whether they are Christians or not. Your parents love you; they know you; and they want the best for you. As you prayerfully consider their instructions for your life, the way you take will be a whole lot easier if you walk respectfully before them, heeding their instructions.

When it comes to choosing a mate, it's not brain surgery to figure out why their counsel in this area is invaluable. First of all, they are not in love with your man, so they can see him objectively. Second, they know and love you, so they are sensitive to what your needs are—what will work for you and what will hinder you. So when they speak on the matter of a mate, you need to treat them like E. F. Hutton and listen!

Samson didn't listen—to either his heavenly Father or his earthly parents. As a matter of fact, he was downright disrespectful.

Basically he told them he knew what he was doing and to butt out. This Philistine woman looked good to him, or, as Young's Literal Translation states, she was "right in [his] eyes," (Judges 14:3, italics mine) so that was the end of that. This is a big no-no. Samson's words would come back to haunt him. Are you convinced yet that you ought to let God do the picking? If not, you will be by the time I'm finished with this story.

ON YOUR MARK, GET SET...

There's another perspective to consider: God's. The Scripture tells us that he was planning to use Samson's situation to deal with the Philistines. Unfortunately, Samson didn't seem concerned about carrying out God's purpose. His mind was not focused on the things of God. He did not see the enemies of God for what they were. He was just going along in life, like many of us, seeking ways to fulfill his fleshly desires, completely ignoring the call of God's Spirit on his life.

When we forget that we were created for God's pleasure, not our own—and that it is in bringing him pleasure that we find it—God usually has to take drastic measures to shape us up. Sometimes he allows something painful to happen in our lives to focus our attention where it ought to be. Such was the case with Samson.

I urge you to choose differently, to walk in purpose because you know it delights the heart of God. Remember that according to God, obedience is better than sacrifice (1 Samuel 15:22). Little did Samson know what he was getting into.

Samson's response to his parents' warning was to intimidate them into silence and compromise to keep the peace between them. We do this to our friends. When we don't like what they say about what we're doing, we either badger them into seeing things our way, or we keep going until we find someone who does.

Agreement is not always a good thing, my sister. Remember: Faithful are the wounds of a friend, but the kisses of an enemy are deceitful (Proverbs 27:6). In other words, those truthful words may hurt, but they come from one who cares enough to warn you about the danger you're in.

If you don't care enough about yourself to heed good advice, well, that's your choice. At the end of the day your demise will be no one's fault but your own. Or, as a childhood saying goes, "A hard head makes a soft behind." Samson had a hard head. But his hard head was affecting others. Not only was he going down, he was taking others down with him.

> Samson went down to Timnah together with his father and mother. As they approached the vineyards of Timnah, suddenly a young lion came roaring toward him. The Spirit of the LORD came upon him in power so that he tore the lion apart with his bare hands as he might have torn a young goat. But he told neither his father nor his mother what he had done. Then he went down and talked with the woman, and he liked her. (Judges 14:5–7)

When you're hardheaded, you ignore signs. Samson was on his way to Timnah to see this woman, and a lion came at him! He killed the lion and then defiled himself by moving the dead body, which was considered unclean according to Jewish law (Leviticus 11:26–28). Scripture makes no mention of his washing his clothing as he should have. Samson had no regard for the Law he had been taught from childhood! He was on a mission. Since he overcame the lion, he thought no more of it and continued on his path.

Let me ask you, who is the lion in our lives? Could it be Satan? I think so. We are told in 1 Peter 5:8 to be self-controlled and alert because the devil is roaming around "like a roaring lion" in search of those he may devour. Did you know he needs our permission to gobble us up? Many a woman is a juicy target. Her desperation to have a man, any man, in her life has left her wide open and unprotected from the devil's jaws. All the signs are there to show that the man in her life is not good for her, but she is not alert or self-controlled, but rather ruled by her longings.

What does the lion look like?

In the last days...people will be lovers of themselves, lovers of money, boastful, proud, abusive, disobedient to their parents, ungrateful, unholy, without love, unforgiving, slanderous, without self-control, brutal, not lovers of the good, treacherous, rash, conceited, lovers of pleasure rather than lovers of God—having a form of godliness but denying its power. Have nothing to do with them.

They are the kind who worm their way into homes and gain control over weak-willed women, who are loaded down with sins and are swayed by all kinds of evil desires, always learning but never able to acknowledge the truth. (2 Timothy 3:2–7)

I've met many a man who falls under one of those descriptions, haven't you? There are plenty of proud, self-centered, pleasure-loving, out-of-control men. And I'm sad to say, a few managed to worm their way into my heart and gain control over my thoughts and actions for a season. And though I had dear friends who confronted me with the truth, I was not able to acknowledge it, so blinded was I by my own desire for the "comfort" of deceptive arms.

So was Samson. Though God extended his grace to Samson when he had that encounter with the lion by strengthening him to overcome it, Samson didn't recognize the dangerous direction in which he was headed. Many times God initially saves us from our mistakes to give us the chance to get back on the right road, but like Samson we forge onward, blind to all the hints heaven is offering us.

I have to say, though, I think Samson had a glimmer something was up. He just wasn't willing to deal with it yet. Why do I say that? Because he became secretive. He lost his transparency. He refused to be accountable to anyone who would tell him the truth in love because he didn't want to hear it. Why didn't he tell his parents about his episode with the lion—especially since he had triumphed over it?

You know the feeling. You and your significant other have intense fellowship (another term for *fight),* or you find out something undesirable about him. You start to suspect the situation you are in is dead, unclean. But you manage to salvage the issue. You don't even bother to bring it up because you know what your friends would say: "You see, I told you something wasn't right about him. You better cut your losses now while you still have something to recover." You don't want to hear that so you just sweep it under the rug and determine that what they don't know won't hurt them. But it might hurt you.

Anyway, Samson visited the Philistine girl and decided he liked her. Whoa! Back up. He liked her based on what? Remember that Judges 14:1 tells us he saw the woman; verse 7 says he talked to the woman and decided he liked her. So he made his initial decision based on flesh. He also made his secondary decision based on flesh, because how much could a conversation tell him? Enough to make an educated decision on the rest of his life with this person? I don't think so. But she looked good to him, and that was enough. That's always enough at first.

Believe it or not, this was only the beginning of Samson's demise. On his way back to marry this woman he stopped to check out the lion he left for dead and discovered that bees had built a nest in the carcass of the lion, and he made another big boo-boo: "He turned aside to look at the lion's carcass. In it was a swarm of bees and some honey, which he scooped out with his hands and ate as he went along. When he rejoined his parents, he gave them some, and they too ate it. But he did not tell them that he had taken the honey from the lion's carcass" (Judges 14:8–9).

Samson was not supposed to touch dead things, yet we find him doing it not once, but twice—on purpose, willfully! This is indicative of serious spiritual decline. If we manage to extract anything sweet from the bad situation we're in, we consider it enough to justify our continued involvement. The thing is dead. It is stinking to high heaven. Everybody else can smell it. They are holding their noses and pointing at the man. But we hold up one little finger covered in honey, kick all of our bad experiences under the rug with our free leg, and say, "But when he's sweet, he's really sweet." When we engage ourselves in dead situations and then pollute others by having them swallow the fruit of our bad decisions, we are on a dangerous road.

I hope I'm not crunching on too many toes here!

THE GAMES PEOPLE PLAY

So our superhero thought he had everybody where he wanted them, and he was feeling good—so good that he stretched his luck by offering up a riddle at his wedding party. If his guests could solve the riddle he would give them each a linen garment and a set of clothes as a prize. If they didn't solve the riddle, they had to give him thirty linen garments and thirty sets of clothes.

The guests were not amused, nor were they clever enough to guess the riddle's answer, so they threatened the bride. Girl, game playing is unedifying. Any time one person starts playing games in a relationship, someone's security is threatened. Guessing should

TOKENS, TRANSFERS, AND PASSES, OH MY!

never be part of the equation in love. It leaves the door open for confusion and strife.

So then we had an insecure bride trying to wheedle the answer out of an uncooperative groom. His silence only heightened her desperation, and before you know it, those familiar words hit their mark: "If you really loved me, you would...." Manipulation had entered the relationship. So Samson shared his secret with her and the downward spiral continued. She told the guests. They answered Samson. He became angry because he knew who told them and that proved excuse enough to go on a murderous tangent.

> Samson said to them,
> "If you had not ploughed with my heifer,
> you would not have solved my riddle."
>
> Then the Spirit of the LORD came upon him in power. He went down to Ashkelon, struck down thirty of their men, stripped them of their belongings and gave their clothes to those who had explained the riddle. Burning with anger, he went up to his father's house. (Judges 14:18–19)

Don't we always go back to the Father, licking our wounds, after we've set ourselves up to be betrayed? Unfortunately, after he has soothed us with healing balm, we begin to romanticize the past and return to where we know we have no business.

> Later on, at the time of wheat harvest, Samson took a young goat and went to visit his wife. He said, "I'm going to my wife's room." But her father would not let him go in.
>
> "I was so sure you thoroughly hated her," he said, "that I gave her to your friend. Isn't her younger sister more attractive? Take her instead."

> Samson said to them, "This time I have a right to get even with the Philistines; I will really harm them." (Judges 15:1–3)

Man! That is cold. His bride went off with Samson's best man. His friend! You know, God will let you get your feelings hurt if you persist in walking outside his will. Samson not only set his heart up for betrayal; he set himself up for rejection.

By the time a situation escalates to these proportions, it's hard to go back to the Father. The pain and the shame are too overwhelming. This is where we begin to simmer in our own juices. Instead of calling on the One who mends broken hearts, we become vengeful in thought, word, or deed, and we begin to justify our bad behavior. We never have the right to curse or carry out vindictive actions against anyone who has hurt us. Anger and bitterness are like cancers that spread rapidly, and in the end more than the intended target gets hit. Negative emotions affect even those you didn't mean to touch. And a vicious cycle of revenge begins.

So then Samson went out, tied the tails of three hundred foxes together, set torches in the tied-up tails, and released the foxes into the fields of the Philistines. This completely destroyed their crops. This was no small task—talk about a lot of time and energy being focused on revenge!

> When the Philistines asked, "Who did this?" they were told, "Samson, the Timnite's son-in-law, because his wife was given to his friend."
>
> So the Philistines went up and burned her and her father to death. Samson said to them, "Since you've acted like this, I won't stop until I get my revenge on you." (Judges 15:6–7)

This time Samson's tirade against the Philistines cost his ex-wife and her father their lives. It also caused the Philistines to turn on those Samson was supposed to protect: the tribes of Israel! Eventually they pleaded with him to turn himself in; he did this, but only after killing a thousand Philistines. Finally the drama subsided for a season.

Now, you would think that Samson would have had his fill of Philistine women, but no! He just decided he wouldn't marry any of them. The next scene finds our fine Nazirite friend at the home of a Philistine prostitute. Was his heart hardened or what? When we don't take our pain to God, our philosophy tends to become "use or be used." Since this is really against our nature as children of God, this attitude sets us up for further trials.

Sure enough, the enemy discovered Samson's whereabouts and gathered to plot his demise. He escaped, but I'm not sure that's a good thing. Those who continue to escape the consequences of their actions start believing there are none. But eventually we all meet our match. Yeah, girl, this is where Delilah came in.

Just when you say, "I can handle it," life hands you a situation that handles you. So Samson decided he wasn't going to marry any more Philistine women, but he wasn't above living with them. When you refuse to learn the lessons that God has been teaching you, you repeat the lesson. Have you dated the same guy in different sizes, shapes, and colors? Have you found yourself on the treadmill of repeat relationships? been subjected to the same cycle of disappointment? wondered why you always attract the same type?

When you forsake purpose and take your desires into your own hands, you leave yourself open to deception. Samson not only entered into a cycle of bad choices and regret, eventually he grew comfortable with sin. The historian Josephus states in his chronicle of Samson's life that he was living with a prostitute called Delilah in the valley of Sorek. Sorek means "choice vines."

The Better to Seduce You With, My Dear

Satan has selected choice vines to wrap up our hearts and squeeze the life out of them before he devours us—if we give him permission. How do we give him permission? By compensating for our disappointments in our own strength instead of returning to the Lord after we've made mistakes. What was a Nazirite priest doing, living with a Philistine prostitute? Drinking wine, and, well, you can just imagine! Last time I checked, Samson wasn't even supposed to eat grapes, never mind drink wine! (Numbers 6:3). Fornication was definitely out of the question. Yet Samson did all of these without a sign of repentance. An unrepentant heart makes a soul lack discernment. Samson didn't even see history getting ready to repeat itself.

> The rulers of the Philistines went to [Delilah] and said, "See if you can lure him into showing you the secret of his great strength and how we can overpower him so we may tie him up and subdue him. Each one of us will give you eleven hundred shekels of silver."
>
> So Delilah said to Samson, "Tell me the secret of your great strength and how you can be tied up and subdued." (Judges 16:5–6)

Duh—doesn't this ring a bell, Samson? Of course not! He thought he was handling it. He gave Delilah a bogus answer. She betrayed him. The Philistines seized him. He escaped—and went back for more! He repeated this exercise three times!

"Why? How?" you exclaim. Girl, for the same reason you keep giving that knuckleheaded man in your life another chance when he has already shown you that he is no good. Samson lacked discernment, and this always leads to bondage, total spiritual blindness, and the death of the relationship. Just death, death, death, spiritually, emotionally, sometimes even physically.

Sure enough, somewhere along the way, against better judgment, Samson became totally vulnerable and exposed the secret of his strength. Satan wants you to expose the secret of your strength, too, and then he can destroy you.

LET IT ALL HANG OUT

Ladies, even a bad man can wear you down if you let him stay around long enough. Your "needs" will override your reason and make you vulnerable. You will expose that which should only be uncovered for the one who has made a life commitment to you.

Notice that Scripture makes no mention of anyone trying to tell Samson anything anymore. They had all given up and gone home, including God. Samson finally told Delilah that he was a Nazirite priest—and that the secret of his strength lay in his hair. Is that so? Perhaps that's what Samson's problem really was. He failed to see who was the true source of his power.

Samson had not spent much time nurturing his relationship with God. Therefore he was religious, trusting in symbols for strength and redemption. Religion has lulled many a single into thinking she has been able to keep herself in her own strength. Samson's strength was not in his hair. His hair was to have been a sign of his being set apart for the purposes of God. But his attitude was that God was around to further Samson's purposes. That led to God's sending a resounding message: "No, I am NOT!"

After Delilah had his head shaved and betrayed him yet again, we read one of the saddest Scriptures in the Bible. It should make us all take a pause for the cause and rethink our romantic alliances.

Then she called, "Samson, the Philistines are upon you!"
He awoke from his sleep and thought, "I'll go out as

before and shake myself free." But he did not know that the LORD had left him.

Then the Philistines seized him, gouged out his eyes and took him down to Gaza. Binding him with bronze shackles, they set him to grinding in the prison. (Judges 16:20–21)

You know the end of the story. Samson's hair grew back, he got another opportunity to punish the Philistines, called on God for strength, and died in a blaze of glory, killing more of his enemies as he died than he did when he was alive. It was a needlessly premature end for a man with great potential that occurred because he had total disregard for his relationship with God. He pursued not God's purpose, but his own.

Girl, let me tell you something. You are not a fool when you make a mistake. You are a fool if you refuse to learn from it. As the saying goes, "The first time, shame on him. The second time, shame on you." What is the lesson here? "Do not give dogs what is sacred; do not throw your pearls to pigs. If you do, they may trample them under their feet, and then turn and tear you to pieces" (Matthew 7:6).

What is sacred? Your heart. Your body. Your vision. Your gifts. Your destiny. These things belong in the hands of God until he places you in front of the one he designed as your partner. If you don't know where you are going, you are destined to get on the wrong bus. You will either end up where you don't want to go, or even worse, you'll find yourself at a dead end with no way out.

If Samson had spent as much time with God as he did with those Philistine women, I'm sure his priorities and his end would have been drastically different. Like Adam naming the animals, Samson would have been able to call the Philistine women what they were: not mate material.

Instead he got stuck in the animal kingdom. Those women did not see his life or his heart as valuable. They trampled on his purpose and ripped his destiny to shreds. Many a woman who has a lot to give has found herself in this predicament—too torn to get back on the road to fulfilling her God-ordained purpose. And many who would have profited from her gifts are left wanting.

Samson died young and left the Israelite nation still in bondage to the Philistines. He allowed sensuality to tear his attention from God's call on his life. He was too distracted by his flesh to nurture his spirit. So let me ask you: Is anybody cutting your hair?

If so, don't blame God when you find your hair all gone. Asking him to take away the desire for the person you've become entangled with is a fruitless prayer. God asks you to make a decision and follow it with action. He instructs us to flee youthly lusts (2 Timothy 2:22). Why are they considered *youthly* lusts? Because they are sinful situations we choose even when we know better, which is childish. To ask God to bless your mess is unacceptable. To blame him for a tragic marriage that you arranged for yourself is ludicrous.

Everything we do must be submitted to God for his approval or it is of no profit. Anything we do from a flesh-motivated stance is doomed to great difficulty or failure—whether we use his name or not. "Unless the LORD builds the house, its builders labor in vain. Unless the LORD watches over the city, the watchmen stand guard in vain" (Psalm 127:1).

Can God really be disappointed in your choice for a mate? Oh, yes! Some choices we make cause God to lean forward on his throne in pain. Why? Because he sees the consequences of our actions before we do.

The Bible states that Ahab was a most evil king. He added to Israel's burden by marrying Jezebel and following her into Baal worship. God considered his marriage to Jezebel worse than all his other evil exploits. In the end her manipulations cost them the kingdom and both their lives.

King Solomon also went after a few foreign women—a thousand, to be exact! I guess he didn't witness to them, because the Bible records that they led his heart away from the Lord and toward idol worship. It cost him dearly. The Lord took the kingdom away from his son, allowing him to remain king over only one tribe because of his promise to David. It was a legacy lost because of bad choices. As I said, the wrong mate can mess up your life.

The blessing of the Lord makes us rich and adds no sorrow (Proverbs 10:22), but the gifts we take for ourselves cost more than we are ever prepared to give. They cause us to sweat and toil in order to secure them, and they never seem to yield what we desire of them. In the heat of our efforts to extract our desire from them, these things become idols.

When we choose mates on our own, minus the counsel of God, they become princes or kings that rule over us. God wants to grant us mates who walk beside us while lovingly leading us. Even a God-ordained marriage can be difficult because marriage crucifies certain areas of our flesh. But just imagine the added difficulty of a marriage that God did not design. No one in her right mind would choose such a hard life on purpose.

God promises that his yoke is easy and his burden is light. With his call, he gives the grace to bear what he asks us to carry. So if you're struggling to make your relationship with a man work more than your relationship with God, if you've dislocated your purpose in search of the perfect mate, you can rest assured you are on your way to a bad haircut.

I suggest that you pull that cord, stand up, and run for the nearest exit. Leave behind all tokens, transfers, and passes. Get off that bus, girl. Run! Do not walk, do not pass go, do not collect two hundred dollars! Head straight back into the arms of your Father until you find your strength renewed.

Dear Heavenly Father, I have made my own choices and failed miserably. Please forgive me. These are such simple words that sound so hollow in the face of all that I have done, yet all I have to offer is a contrite heart. I pray that you will receive me and restore me.

I must confess that somewhere along the way I lost the joy of my salvation and believed that your love was not enough to sustain me. I went in search of poor replacements and found my soul shipwrecked on the rocks of my own willfulness. And now, with my wounds still fresh, I've made my way back to you.

I apologize for bringing you such a poor offering. I long for the day when I won't come before you this way, but willingly, joyfully, from love for you and only you. Restore my sight. Renew my hunger for you. Stir within me the longing to do your will.

Teach me to love you. Let the love I have for you remove all other princes and idols from my heart. Let no man have dominion over my soul, my mind, my body. Draw me close to yourself and consume me with your presence. Love all the hurt away from my heart.

As I place my life and my heart back into your hands, make me whole in you and you alone, in Jesus' name. Amen.

SIX

TAKING THE EXPRESS ROUTE

He who finds a wife finds a good thing,
And obtains favor from the LORD.
PROVERBS 18:22, NASB

N ow that you've gotten off the wrong bus, how do you get on the right one? How do you get God to whisper in the ear of your husband-to-be that it is time to make that move? How do you get off the twisting trail and onto the express route? How do you become the "favor" that special man obtains?

You achieve these things by becoming blessed and highly favored yourself. Only one woman is recorded in the history of the Bible who was described this way. She was a single woman by the name of Mary. She was engaged to a young carpenter when certain life-changing events took place that, in my opinion, affirm the high regard that God has for his singles.

You know the story. We rehearse it every Christmas, but I suggest you take another look at the details in light of Mary's personality and God's choice of her as mother of his Son. I think it's time for us to check out her secrets.

"In the sixth month, God sent the angel Gabriel to Nazareth, a town in Galilee, to a virgin pledged to be married to a man named Joseph, a descendant of David. The virgin's name was Mary. The angel went to her and said, 'Greetings, you who are highly favored! The Lord is with you'" (Luke 1:26–28).

First, notice that the Lord was *with* Mary, which meant that she was with him. The Word tells us that if we draw near to God, he will draw near to us (James 4:8). To whom are you drawing near?

One of the definitions of being cursed is to be held in contempt and disregarded by God; the opposite of that is to be blessed by having the regard of God on our lives. This is when God turns his attention our way and makes his favor and presence known in our lives. The way he does this is to bless us with the ability to be fruitful! He blesses the fruit of our womb, he causes the works of our hands to prosper. He makes our relationships rich and prosperous spiritually, emotionally, and physically. When God does this, he is reversing what took place in the Garden. These were the three areas affected by the curse: the womb, productivity, and relationships.

Obviously Mary was a worshiper who had a very special and intimate relationship with God. It was so intimate that she was sensitive enough in the Spirit to be able to see the angel and receive what he had to say. This came from pursuing the presence of God. Mary took time to set herself apart from others to seek God's face. Small wonder there was something about her attitude and countenance that God liked, something that caused him to want to draw close and extend favor to her.

Let's think about favor for a minute. If a stranger walked up to you on the street and said, "Do me a favor, loan me a hundred dollars," would you give it to him? Of course not! You don't know this person. You don't know where he lives. You have no references. You have no history to go on, nothing to nurture trust. You don't know his intentions because you know nothing about his character.

Favor is reliant on relationship. We do favors for those we know and trust. The more intimate the relationship is, the greater the favor that we are willing to give. Yes, it is clear that Mary had an intimate relationship with the Lord.

The great evidence of this was her faith in what the Lord said, as impossible as it sounded. Elizabeth told Mary that she was blessed because she believed what the Lord had told her would be accomplished. Only when you have a close relationship with someone do you dare to believe everything he says.

BODY LANGUAGE

Mary had another special characteristic. She was a virgin. Mary walked in purity before God. This was pleasing to him. She worshiped him in Spirit and in truth. She presented her body to him as a living sacrifice, holy and acceptable. She understood that her body was a temple of worship unto the Lord. Though she was engaged, she had never known a man. She had kept herself unto the day of her marriage. She belonged to the Lord first, her future husband second. To whom does your body belong?

Now, if you're not a virgin, don't fall into condemnation. I mentioned this in a previous chapter, but I want to elaborate here. If you have confessed your past mistakes to God, know that he has given you a new beginning. It is up to you, however, to maintain your renewed purity: "Do not go on presenting the members of your body to sin as instruments of unrighteousness; but present yourselves to God as those alive from the dead, and your members as instruments of righteousness to God" (Romans 6:13, NASB).

Mary presented her body to God as an instrument of righteousness, and he honored her presentation with a special blessing. If you are feeling you can't be God's vessel because you once used your body for your own pleasure instead of God's glory, again, don't fall for the deception of the enemy. God checks our hearts to find purity, and he is pleased to abide in a heart that has cleansed itself in the blood of Jesus and rinsed itself off in the rivers of repentance. He has hurled your sin as far as the east is from the west to remember it no more (Psalm 103:12; Jeremiah 31:34). You are free to begin again, to be counted as a candidate for being used by God to do great and wonderful things.

Does that sound too wonderful? Even Mary could not fathom being selected for such an incredible blessing. It is a humbling thing to know that God has turned and looked your way, though his eyes are upon us all twenty-four hours a day, seven days a week. Yeah child, he's watching us all the time, watching over his treasured possession.

You may wonder why this sex thing is so important. Why is fornication adultery in the eyes of God? Why is he so fussy about what you do with your body? Because your body belongs to him!

Yet the body is not for immorality, but for the Lord; and the Lord is for the body....

Do you not know that your bodies are members of Christ? Shall I then take away the members of Christ and make them members of a harlot? May it never be!

Or do you not know that the one who joins himself to a harlot is one body with her? For He says, "The two will become one flesh."

But the one who joins himself to the Lord is one spirit with Him.

Flee immorality. Every other sin that a man commits is outside the body, but the immoral man sins against his own body.

Or do you not know that your body is a temple of the

Holy Spirit who is in you, whom you have from God, and
that you are not your own?

For you have been bought with a price: therefore glorify God in your body. (1 Corinthians 6:13, 15–20, NASB)

Oh my! This is serious. Your body does not belong to you. It
belongs to your fiancé and husband, Jesus Christ. Yes! Every single
one of you is actually already spoken for, already engaged to the
ultimate Bridegroom, Jesus himself. He has already paid the dowry
for you. He expects you to keep your body for him, or for the one
he has chosen to use to manifest his love to you. When you choose
your own partner outside the boundaries of matrimony, you are
literally cheating on God! And get this, ladies—your Husband is
watching while you cheat on him.

Oh, it goes even deeper. You are also allowing the Holy Spirit,
who abides within you, to be violated. Intimacy without consent
is rape. The Holy Spirit will not consent to sex outside of marriage.
Therefore you subject the Holy Spirit to something totally against
his nature. Remember, the Holy Spirit is a person too. He is real,
living, breathing, and inside of you, and he's trying to assist you in
walking in holiness, in glorifying God. Let him do his work.

So, let's see. Who would have thought one little physical act
could have so many deep ramifications: adultery, violation, and
last but certainly not least, bondage? You create a soul tie with the
one you join yourself to. You become a slave to the man you surrender to. Eew!

This is why God calls those who partake in sex outside of marriage, with no accountability to him, prostitutes. The body of a
prostitute is not her own. A body not in submission to God has
sold itself out to be pimped by Satan himself. Just because that
woman thinks she is behaving of her own free will does not mean
she is free. She is actually deceived and totally unaware that she

has merely surrendered to one who will collect from her physically, emotionally, and spiritually.

In the end those who persist in premarital sex are left feeling empty, spent, and betrayed. Their self-esteem is ripped to shreds; their relationship with God is in question in their own minds; and the pall of resignation that rejection is to be their lot in life is wrapped around them like a wet blanket.

And can we discuss the pain of a severed relationship once you've slept with someone? No matter how you work it out intellectually, the wound penetrates much deeper than skin because you've bonded your soul to this person. Sex is not just a physical act. It is a spiritual one. It is the ultimate surrender. It is associated with worship in many cultures. This is why sex was a part of pagan worship before gods and idols. When you give totally of yourself to another human being, only to be rejected, you are left naked and ashamed, bleeding spiritually, as this person yanks a layer off of your spirit and leaves you to die in your own pain. Then we turn back to our Husband and ask him to heal us. Thank God he doesn't respond to us the same way we would respond to an unfaithful lover.

Do you still refuse to believe that God associates your keeping your body with worshiping him? Think of it this way: To give your body to another without God's approval is to set your desire for that person above him. That is idolatry. And you know he doesn't like that, 'cause he's a jealous Lover. And after all he's done for us, he's earned the right to be jealous. If you gave your life for someone and then he went off with somebody else, you'd be upset too. Hopefully you're getting God's point.

Check this out: "Do not be deceived; neither fornicators, nor idolaters, nor adulterers, nor effeminate, nor homosexuals, nor thieves, nor the covetous, nor drunkards, nor revilers, nor swindlers, shall inherit the kingdom of God" (1 Corinthians 6:9–10, NASB).

Isn't that interesting? Look at the list. Fornication, idolatry, and adultery are linked together! Idolatry follows fornication, adultery follows that, and then other sexual sins are listed. Before you ever get to inheriting the kingdom of God, let's talk about kingdom living right here on earth. You know, just the stuff that everybody wants: a little righteousness, peace, and joy in the Holy Ghost. That's not much to ask, is it? Well, that is totally up to us. It is impossible to experience right standing with God, any degree of peace of mind, or lasting joy, when we are in disobedience to God. It opens the door for us to become victims, used and discarded, once those lovers have had their fill of us. This is not God's plan for our lives.

For those who choose to justify physical intimacy by saying they are already married in the spirit because they are in a committed relationship or engaged, remember, it ain't over till the lady, fat or thin, sings at the church. Okay? You have no guarantees.

Let me ask this question. How much is your love worth to you? How much is your life worth to you? Only you can answer those two questions. If you're facing temptations in the sexual arena, forget about yourself and remember that your body belongs to God, so watch how you treat his possession.

Though Mary was engaged, she did not release her body to her betrothed, but continued to keep herself in honor to God as an act of worship to him. As a matter of fact, Joseph did not touch Mary until after she had given birth to Jesus.

MATCHMAKER, MAKE ME A MATCH

Speaking of Joseph, he was no spare tire in this scenario. His role was just as pivotal. He was a God-ordained, handpicked special. How do I know? Because the Bible is careful to state his lineage. He was a descendant of David, remember? This is important because God had promised David that the scepter would never depart from David's lineage; therefore Joseph was selected to be the earthly father of the King of kings and Lord of lords. Do you see how this is all working together here?

How could Mary have kept up with all of these details? She couldn't have. She didn't have all the information about her future. But God did. He has all the information about your future too. He knows how many children you will have and even whom their lives will affect. He knows everything about everything! So how can you be the one who selects your mate? You don't know what's coming your way!

Needless to say, mate selection is critical when it comes to being able to perpetuate God's overall kingdom plan. The right teams have to be in place to carry out what he has purposed from the beginning.

If you are a woman whom God has called like Esther, for "such a time as this," it is important for you to have a husband who understands that. You will need a man who can hear from God and lead you into the fullness of your calling. A man who is not sensitive to the Holy Spirit could shut down all of your spiritual stuff, and you would have to cooperate because he is your head.

Let's think about the situation in Luke. Here Mary said yes to God about carrying his child. But what was Joseph going to have to say about that? This was a dangerous decision on Mary's part. How do you go to your fiancé and say, "Baby, I'm going to have the Son of God"? Can you imagine the reaction? "What drug are you on? Now who's the *real* father?"

Many a woman has been asked that question when telling the father of her child that she is expecting. To be pregnant out of wedlock in Mary's day bore some serious consequences. She would be accused of fornication, declared unclean, and stoned to death. This proves she was truly sold out to God: She was willing to risk death in order to do his will. She was ready to withstand public opinion and scrutiny, even false accusation, rejection, and a death sentence, if it came to that. Joseph himself could have grown indignant at her announcement and shouted, "Off with her head!" But he did not. There was something about Mary that restrained him from impulsive action. He knew what God knew about Mary—that she was a godly woman. So her confession troubled him. He was a torn man.

On one hand, Joseph knew that Mary would never behave in an ungodly fashion. On the other hand, how did she get pregnant? Though he struggled, he could not get past Mary's godly reputation.

What is your reputation? Would a man argue on your behalf if he heard a negative rumor about you? Or would he think that what he heard was a possibility?

Mary's reputation put Joseph in a quandary. It was hard for him to accept this idea of an angel and a God-inspired pregnancy. After all, it had never happened before! The natural explanation made so much more sense. So with heavy heart and troubled mind, Joseph pondered breaking off the engagement privately and concealing the matter.

Because Joseph her husband was a righteous man and did not want to expose her to public disgrace, he had in mind to divorce her quietly.

But after he had considered this, an angel of the Lord appeared to him in a dream and said, "Joseph son of David, do not be afraid to take Mary home as your wife, because what is conceived in her is from the Holy Spirit. She will give birth to a son, and you are to give him the name Jesus, because he will save his people from their sins."

When Joseph woke up, he did what the angel of the

Lord had commanded him and took Mary home as his
wife. (Matthew 1:19–21, 24)

What if Joseph had been out of the Spirit and reacted in the
flesh? God's plan would have suffered violent repercussions! But
Joseph was sensitive to the Holy Spirit. God told him to marry
Mary!

Will you allow God to speak to your husband-to-be on your
behalf? Will you let him be the one to contact and assign the man
for your life?

When God speaks to the man that he has chosen for you, he
will also instill in that man a sense of purpose for your union.
Joseph heard God's voice clearly and was obedient. He did not get
sensitive and start feeling insecure. He did not allow the situation
to emasculate him. He graciously took his place beside Mary in this
very special assignment.

Notice that God told Joseph what to name Jesus, establishing
his role as earthly father and spiritual head. God let Joseph know
in no uncertain terms that his presence was significant in the
scheme of things. He was to provide for Mary and Jesus. He was to
be their leader and their cover. Once Mary and Joseph were married, it was to Joseph that God addressed his instruction for the
family. He was to be the responsible, designated driver.

When they had gone, an angel of the Lord appeared to
Joseph in a dream. "Get up," he said, "take the child and
his mother and escape to Egypt. Stay there until I tell you,
for Herod is going to search for the child to kill him."

So he got up, took the child and his mother during
the night and left for Egypt.

After Herod died, an angel of the Lord appeared in a
dream to Joseph in Egypt and said, "Get up, take the child

and his mother and go to the land of Israel, for those who
were trying to take the child's life are dead."

So he got up, took the child and his mother and went
to the land of Israel. (Matthew 2:13–14, 19–21)

Give me a man who listens to God! It's a matter of life and death!
This brings us back to another facet of Mary's personality.
Mary trusted God completely. She told Joseph her situation and
left him in the hands of God as she left to visit her cousin Elizabeth.
She allowed God to speak on her behalf. She didn't waste time trying to convince him that he should do right by her, feel sorry for
her, be responsible for her. She did not try to manipulate him with
her pregnancy. She simply stated her case and moved on. She was
willing to sacrifice even her fiancé to birth the purposes of God.

Are you willing to surrender all to God in order to see his purposes manifested in your world? Mary was. Check her response to
the angel: "'I am the Lord's servant,' Mary answered. 'May it be to
me as you have said.' Then the angel left her" (Luke 1:38).

WANTED: AVAILABLE WOMEN

I have two last points about Mary. Mary was single and completely
submitted—available to be used by her heavenly Father. She was
submitted to God, to his plan for her life, to her husband, to her
role as a mother. What God can do with a submitted woman is
beyond our comprehension. The things that can be produced
from the life of a single woman submitted to the call of God will
blow your mind. I am a living witness.

Nothing mattered more to Mary than what God desired from
her—not Joseph or the opinion of her loved ones. For God and
God alone she lived, in order to see the fulfillment of his promise
to Israel.

What is your motivation for what you do? Is it all about you, or all about God? Does your heart beat for your own purposes or for the purposes of God?

By now you should know that true joy and fulfillment are found only in the center of God's divine purposes for your life. Any married person can tell you a mate is not what makes one happy. It is landing right smack-dab in the middle of the purpose you were created for that inflates the heart and gives you a sense of well-being all your days. Mary was determined to stand up to the challenge.

Mary also submitted to her husband, Joseph. Though she had a very special "ministry," she yielded to her husband's leadership. She didn't put her hand on her hip and say, "I'm not going to Egypt! I just had the Son of God! God speaks to me too! He didn't tell me anything about going to Egypt. That's not where my ministry is. I want to go back home and show my baby off to my friends and family. Stop stifling me."

Mm-mm, she didn't do that. She followed Joseph's lead. Her submission saved their lives. Even at her young and tender age, Mary understood that submission is not about being a doormat. It is about putting oneself in a position to be blessed. Take a clue from Mary.

Mary also understood that as a mother she was to remain submitted to God's plan for her child's life. She was to raise her son, continually pointing him toward the Father, instilling a sense of purpose and destiny into his young life. This called for releasing him on her part. She did not raise Jesus to be a Mama's boy. She raised Jesus to release him to the world. She didn't yank him out of the temple and tell him to go play like the other children. She understood that his future required his knowledge of the Father. She was the one to encourage Jesus to perform his first miracle. And she watched him go to the cross.

Mary lived with her hands open to God's putting in or taking away whatever he pleased. She claimed nothing as her own—not her life, not her desires, not her marriage, not her son.

Are your hands open? What are you clinging to? Have you been able to keep the things you grasp so tightly, or do they seem to seep between the cracks of your life and escape anyway?

It's time to open your hands and release your life to the One who will always love you most. Only as we become totally available to him will all our dreams come true and our desires be birthed. Only then will we find ourselves on the express route. Only then will our lives become blessed and highly favored.

And blessed and highly favored people can't help but bless others. And so our fulfillment becomes complete.

Dear Heavenly Father, I have been grasping my life tightly in my hands, so tightly that it hurts. Help me to release all that I am and all that I have to you.

This is a scary thought to me. I don't quite know what to expect. I confess my distrust of your plan for my life, though I seem to have no better plans of my own. I struggle between my desire to be in the center of your will and my desire to have my own way. Help me to turn my heart toward your desires and design.

I want to trust you more. I want to be excited about your plans. Reveal your heart to me and draw me closer to you. As I tentatively reach out to you, establish my trust in your desire toward me. Ignite passion in my heart for you and your purposes.

Build up my spirit and grant me the will to crucify my flesh. Teach me to be a vessel of worship filled with only you.

Impregnate me with kingdom purpose. Make my heart beat with a sense of destiny that reaches beyond my personal longings.

Strengthen my spirit to long after you and your will above all things. Lord, I make myself totally available to you now. Overtake me, fill me, and use me for your glory, in Jesus' name. Amen.

Was it something I said?
    something I did?
or was my rejection
    predetermined by the fact that I was simply me?
      the wrong one
        in the wrong place
          at the wrong time
   obviously in the wrong frame of mind
      based on my wrong opinion
        that you were right for me
    somewhere along the way
      what started as a pleasant journey
        took us somewhere foreign
      incomprehensible
        indiscernible
          it's hard to say when we took a wrong turn
      nevertheless it happened
        but so lost were we
          in one another's arms
        no one noticed
     until it was too late
      to save our hearts from pain
        our names from shame
          our hopes from being disappointed
     and not being willing to
        share equal parts in the mistake
        we chose to blame one another
          for not taking better care of our hearts
     denying all the while
        that perhaps we both made wrong assumptions
          while being distracted
          by the chemistry that got in the way

causing us to be shortsighted
in the midst of the smoke
hard truths became fuzzy
blurring the road before us for far too long
before it became crystal clear
that we had done
the wrong thing...

THE RIGHT MOVES

SEVEN

CHECKING OUT THE SCENERY

The man said,
"This is now bone of my bones and flesh of my flesh."
GENESIS 2:23

Now that you're in the right place at the right time, you're ready to learn the right moves. So how do you catch the right bus? Simple: You take only the bus that's headed in the right direction.

In biblical days this was a much easier process. Did you ever notice that there was no dating in the Bible? People just got married! How did this happen? The parents selected the mates. The bridegroom's family found a bride for the son. The father then negotiated to secure the deal.

What was the selection based on? Family background, similarities in ethics and values, the personal characteristics of their son and future daughter-in-law. The family decided that if two people were raised in a similar fashion and had comparable values, they would stand a better chance of getting along for the long term.

This method must have had great merit as it seems that the marriages of old stood the test of time far better than our present-day ones do. Even in our day, generally speaking, arranged marriages fare better than our freestyle unions. This leads me to a couple of conclusions. First, we must allow our heavenly Father to do the picking. And second, the decision for a mate must be made on a spiritual and intellectual basis before it's made on an emotional one.

"What about *love?*" you ask. "Why not let the heart and all those mushy feelings show you the way, Michelle?" All right, all you hopeless romantics, I heard that. I'll tell you why: "The heart is deceitful above all things and beyond cure. Who can understand it?" (Jeremiah 17:9).

Every woman has a sorry story to tell about a man whom her heart selected. The heart does not listen to reason and should not be allowed to lead in decision making. Whenever you meet a man, you need to get clearance from God, check out his attributes, and *then* allow your heart to engage. If your heart jumps into the pool before finding out if there's any water in it, you've just subjected yourself to a needless and potentially painful, even deadly, exercise. And if God says no, the whole thing is a waste of time. Remember my earlier reference to unauthorized marriages? Jesus compared good works not advocated by him as unstable—having no foundation—even as sin! Why? Because these things were performed from a self-centered agenda.

Many will say to me on that day, "Lord, Lord, did we not prophesy in your name, and in your name drive out demons and perform many miracles?" Then I will tell them plainly, "I never knew you. Away from me, you evildoers!"

Therefore everyone who hears these words of mine

and puts them into practice is like a wise man who built
his house on the rock. The rain came down, the streams
rose, and the winds blew and beat against that house; yet
it did not fall, because it had its foundation on the rock.
But everyone who hears these words of mine and does
not put them into practice is like a foolish man who built
his house on sand. The rain came down, the streams rose,
and the winds blew and beat against that house, and it fell
with a great crash. (Matthew 7:22–27)

Another translation says, "I never knew you. Go away; the
things you did were unauthorized" (Matthew 7:22, NLT). "Ooh! So
you mean a good thing can be considered sin, Michelle?" Yes, if
God didn't sanction it. Though the context here is the works of
those who claimed to know Christ, yet performed miracles for
their own glory, the same principle applies to a self-generated
union. A marriage that God has not ordained and sanctioned is
more susceptible to difficulties so numerous only a miracle could
save it. When the storms of life prevail against that household, the
couple involved is left attempting to hold a marriage together that
has no foundation. And while their struggle in the flesh to pull it
together usually proves fruitless, God calls them to honor the commitments they made and the vows that they uttered.

Therefore, girlfriend, the unauthorized marriage leaves you
open to almost certain disaster. As I mentioned in chapter 5, King
Ahab married a woman God did not approve of, and she cost him
his life and the legacy of his kingdom. Solomon also married
women God had warned against. This damaged his relationship
with God and cost his sons their inheritance—namely the kingdom. Samson—well, you know that story. The wrong wife was the
beginning of his demise.

WHAT IF I BLOW IT?

There are no easy answers when you realize you've made a bad decision. If you marry someone who isn't God's choice, once you've committed your life to him in the presence of God and earthly witnesses, you can't just throw up your hands and say, "Oops! I made a boo-boo!" You can't easily walk away from the one you promised to stand with for richer or poorer, in sickness and health, till death do you part. Yet the good news is, no matter how hopeless a situation looks, with God's help, it can be salvaged. But do you really want to do the work required to make that happen? This is where most people bottom out, unable to endure the heat of the battle.

My suggestion is a simple one: Clean up the order of your decision-making process and save yourself the trouble on the front end. A marriage that God has ordained will have its own share of struggles simply because two willful human beings are involved. Don't make your life any harder than it has to be.

A famous magazine editor once said she decided early in life that she was not going to marry a poor man. Therefore she refused to even date men who weren't wealthy. She strategically positioned herself to work for wealthy men. She even saved up all her money to buy an expensive car to draw their attention. Her rationale? It was just as easy to fall in love with a poor man as it was to fall in love with a wealthy one. Therefore she would not even allow herself the opportunity to do so accidentally.

That might be an extreme example, but it proves the point Jeremiah made: The heart is willful and is driven by its own agenda. It does not consider things rationally and intelligently—it just loves to love! Therefore you have to point it in the right direction: "Above all else, guard your heart, for it is the wellspring of life" (Proverbs 4:23).

IT'S ALL IN THE FABRIC

Yeah girl, when you want to select a mate, there is a lot more to consider than chemistry. In my book *Secrets of an Irresistible Woman*, I mention the fact that dating exists not for mating; it exists for collecting data. I believe that the biblical design would be friendship, courtship, and then marriage. Friendship is two people walking together in agreement and accountability, learning and growing together. Courtship follows the mutual agreement to commit to one another exclusively—it is the decisive turning toward the agreed-upon goal of the marriage altar. It is a period of laying a foundation and preparing for your life together after marriage. But dating? Well, if you do date, use the time wisely to gather facts.

Though it is important to like the man, love him, and be in love, all those feelings must be based on cumulative information. So take a deep breath, grab a notepad, and let's start at the beginning. I like to compare dating to clothes shopping, so I see three elements that we must examine. First, we must check out the *fabric*. Is this person mate material?

The first thing on the list is—yeah girl, you guessed it—does this man have a relationship with God? Notice I did not ask whether he was "spiritual," "religious," "saved," or "born again," or whether he goes to church. Wait a minute! Pull those eyebrows back down; stop clutching your pearls and wondering if I'm a true believer. I am a blood-bought, blood-washed, redeemed-by-the-blood-of-the-Lamb follower of Jesus Christ of Nazareth. But all of those catchphrases I listed get tossed around a bit too casually these days. So I repeat my question: Does this man have an intimate relationship with the Father through Jesus Christ? Does he care what God thinks about his behavior? Is he accountable to God as well as another colaborer in the faith? Accountability is an important factor. It is imperative to maintaining a committed relationship.

Follow Abraham's example. Look for someone with the same foundation you have.

> [Abraham] said to the chief servant in his household, the one in charge of all that he had, "Put your hand under my thigh. I want you to swear by the LORD, the God of heaven and the God of earth, that you will not get a wife for my son from the daughters of the Canaanites, among whom I am living, but will go to my country and my own relatives and get a wife for my son Isaac." (Genesis 24:2–4)

Is your potential spouse a member of the same family—the family of God? Listen, girl—if you find yourself perfectly at peace about pursuing a relationship with a man who is not walking in the light, I have to question where you stand. Scripture is clear on this point: "Do not be yoked together with unbelievers. For what do righteousness and wickedness have in common? Or what fellowship can light have with darkness?" (2 Corinthians 6:14).

Please note, however, that you must have more in common with the man you are considering for a mate than a relationship with Jesus. Jesus is the cord that can hold you together, but there must be something there to be held together in the first place. You need to have common interests and values and agree on the essentials of living day to day.

This is where being "like" comes in. Remember that when Adam was naming the animals, he noticed they all had a mate of "like" kind. Being of "like" kind means you are compatible in many ways. You have a similar spiritual walk. You eat the same diet. You enjoy a lot of similar things. You have like interests, like goals in life, like opinions on basic life issues. You have had like experiences in your background. Though there is some truth to the idiom that opposites attract, like-minded folks fare better together.

After all, why do you have the friends you have? Because you share like interests and views. Well, marriage is one of the longest and most important friendships you will ever have. Be realistic. Don't make plans to change the man into someone more like you. Make honest assessments of how much you two agree and decide if you could live with this person "as is" for the rest of your life.

TAKING THE SURE COURSE

Now, here's the next question. Does he want to get married? If you want to be married and your dreamboat isn't interested, don't waste your time. That's like getting on a plane headed for Los Angeles when you really want to go to Chicago. You won't get there.

Have you ever noticed the pattern? Women fall in love and get married. Men decide to get married and then look for a wife. Do you see the difference in order? So if a guy says he's not looking for anything serious, take his words seriously. If he is not going your direction, get off that bus and wait for the right one. Don't go along for the ride and then whine later that he led you on. In reality, you ignored the signs and led yourself on by thinking he would eventually turn in your direction. Instead he ran over your heart and left skid marks on your self-esteem.

Here's another even greater question: Does this man want you? Is he pursuing you? I have to tell you, I have been disturbed to receive letters from readers outlining how they positioned themselves to meet men. They put out incredible fleeces to determine whether the Lord was directing a relationship their way. They went through all kinds of back roads and winding trails to figure out if a certain man was "the one" for them. They could have taken the express route. Let's make this plain now: I don't think, I *know* that if you have to ask, the answer is already clear. He is not the one. The man who is right for you will pursue you, and God's hand in the relationship will be clear. No guessing, no fleeces, no dead ends.

Scripture says: "He who finds a wife finds what is good and receives favor from the LORD" (Proverbs 18:22). Who finds whom? All together now: *The man finds the wife.* Just because you don't see a man in your surroundings doesn't mean he isn't there. In the book of Genesis, Jacob went to another land to find his bride. Abraham sent his servant to his relatives' region to bring back Rebekah for Isaac. Ruth left Moab and moved to Israel in order to be found by Boaz. From the beginning of time God has transported men and women across the world in order to put them together. At the right time—let me say that again—at the right time he will bring that man on the scene, and he will find you.

Until then, take a chill pill. You don't need a bunch of men in your life to make you feel all right about yourself. You need only one man—your man, the one God has selected to select you. And trust me, the right man at the wrong time can be just as awful as the wrong man at any time. So trust God's timing in this. He is the ultimate matchmaker. Relax, sit pretty, and allow yourself to be found.

Does that sound too simple? Do you think you ought to be doing something about getting this marriage thing together? Do you feel like life is passing by too quickly for you to wait on God?

Girlfriend, I don't care what year it is. The spirits of a man and a woman are still the same as God created them in the beginning. In God's perfect design, the man is the one who recognizes his mate. Adam had no problem recognizing that Eve was his missing rib. You do not need to strategically place yourself anywhere. You do not have to help a guy out because he's shy.

"But, Michelle, I think he lost my phone number. He's still suffering from the pain of a past relationship. He didn't get a clear signal that I was interested."

These are just excuses you use to justify your desire to help this man understand that you are the one. It's so simple: If he doesn't feel an urgency to know and pursue you, he's not the bus for you. Men do whatever they have to do to get what they truly want.

Look: "Jacob served seven years to get Rachel, but they seemed like only a few days to him because of his love for her" (Genesis 29:20). Hell-o! That's what I'm talking about! When a man wants you, nothing will deter him from his pursuit of you. When he doesn't want you, guess what, ladies? He just doesn't, no matter how wonderful you are. If his heart doesn't choose you, you will spend the rest of your days running after his love, even if you manage to squeeze a marriage vow from his lips. Commitment from obligation is sad and loveless. Leah found that out the hard way.

You remember the story in the book of Genesis. From their first meeting, Jacob loved Rachel. He arranged with her father, Laban, to earn her hand in marriage by working for him seven years. But Laban deceived Jacob, and on the wedding night, he slipped Leah into Jacob's tent. Then he had the nerve to demand that Jacob work another seven years for Rachel! So Jacob was stuck with two wives—one he loved, and one he didn't.

When Leah married Jacob, she got a husband, but in name only. Jacob chose Rachel from the moment he saw her. Being tricked into marrying Leah didn't change his mind. Though Jacob honored his commitment to Leah, his heart condition did not change. He did not rest until he had acquired Rachel's hand also. And Rachel was the one who kept his affections: "[Jacob] loved Rachel more than Leah. And he worked for Laban another seven years" (Genesis 29:30).

The man in your life should recognize you as the pearl of great price in his life and be willing to do whatever he must in order to gain your hand. If he is passive about gaining your affections, take it as a sign that he is not interested. Many a woman's mother has suggested that it is a good idea to marry a man who loves you more than you love him. As cold as that sounds, it actually might be scriptural if you stop to think about it: "We love him because he first loved us" (1 John 4:19).

Jesus, the ultimate Bridegroom, loves us more than we will ever be able to love him. In our mortal frame we don't possess the capacity to love him the way he deserves to be loved. Yet he loves us in spite of ourselves and our earthly limitations. His love for us covers our imperfections. No matter what we think of ourselves, Jesus still finds us desirable. He still longs for us to be by his side. Why? Because we are his choice. We didn't choose him. He chose us.

This translates to our relationship with a natural man as well. When a man chooses you, his love for you will cover your imperfections. As far as he is concerned, once he has captured his prize, you are the best thing since whipped butter. He will constantly celebrate his love victory.

But if you do the choosing, you will spend a lifetime working to convince him he made a good choice. That is too much work, and it's something God never intended for you to do.

FRIENDS AND LOVERS

This is why it is important that you don't make impulsive decisions on whether a man is for you upon your initial meeting. Chemistry isn't enough. And this is why I don't like the concept of dating. If you're dating someone, you're under pressure to choose a direction for your relationship. Walking in friendship and learning about one another with no intimacy involved affords you the opportunity to learn about the character of a man without having to make any snap decisions. Once you have walked together for a while and realize that you share a lot in common, you will feel your hearts bonding, and then you will naturally enter into courtship with the intention of solidifying a commitment.

And again, wait until the man voices his intentions. He should take the lead in establishing the relationship. You may have an inkling that he is the one, but God will use the man to set the tone of the relationship. Allow him the opportunity to woo you—this is your first act of submission. Jesus sets the standard for all men to follow. They should love us first. And they should lead the relationship.

Not only should they recognize us as a valuable addition to their lives, they should "come correct," as they say in the world. Jesus told his disciples, "I go to prepare a place for you. And if I go and prepare a place for you, I will come again, and receive you unto Myself; that where I am, there you may be also" (John 14:2–3, NASB). Jesus has gone to prepare a place where his bride can live. He has anticipated the future and made provision. In biblical days, the groom prepared a home for his bride before he was able to receive her. He either cashed in his inheritance early or worked to build a home for his fiancée. I think the women of today could take a clue. Following the example of Jesus, the man in your life should not desire to move into your house, only into your heart. A man who prepares for your future has made his intentions clear. A man who is husband material has the means to take care of a wife. He is a responsible human being who understands he needs to have something to offer.

In case I sound materialistic here, let me be clear: I am not recommending that you look for a guy who's well-endowed financially. But this is an area where sober consideration cannot be replaced by romanticism. At the age of twenty a man with potential is a beautiful thing. You should anticipate growing together and building a life together. But at the age of forty-two, a man with potential but no actual accomplishments is no longer so attractive.

By this time, a man should be more established in his purpose. Take a man's status in his career goals, his ability to provide, into account when you are considering him. Be fair, but be objective.

In short, a man should have the means to be a suitable cover for you. I find it interesting how quickly women are willing to embrace a man as a partner who shows no capacity to be a responsible husband. Yet if these same women got on a plane and were informed that the pilot had never been formally trained and was unqualified to fly the plane, they would get off. This is your life we're talking about! Make sure the man you say "I do" to is qualified to be a husband.

And girl, check out his buddies. "I don't like his friends!" is one of the most telling remarks about a relationship. Everyone knows birds of a feather flock together, yet most women fail to see the connection between a man and his friends. A man's pals tell you a lot about the person that you haven't seen yet. They reveal things about the guy's character that might be hidden when he is on good behavior. Everyone knows how to put his best foot forward. Don't stay focused on the foot—check out the rest of the body! The bottom line is that a man is like his friends—that is why they are his friends. So his friends speak crudely? So does he—when he is not with you.

And what about his relationship with his mom? How does he treat her? This is your preview of how he will treat you. There are lots of men who, because of a negative relationship with their mothers, really don't like women, yet say they do. Unresolved issues between mother and son continue between husband and wife.

Remember that a man's family reveals the cloth from which he's cut. Take note and decide whether you want your future with the man in your life to look like his present family situation. If you see bitterness and hostility between him and his parents or siblings, count on seeing it between the two of you if you marry.

Examine the fabric closely. Check out the patterns of his life. Do you see repeated cycles of drama in his personal kingdom? broken relationships? problems in making commitments, including to the job market? mood swings? Is a problem always someone else's fault? Does he embrace responsibility or shirk it? Does he keep his promises? Is he a man of good reputation?

Remember, all garments look wonderful hanging in the store, but with wear, some begin to unravel. Give yourself the time and space to check out the man in your life. Time will always reveal whether or not he is made of the right stuff.

IF THE SUIT FITS, WEAR IT

Say you've completed a thorough evaluation of your man and the fabric is good. But what about the fit? Ever bought a suit that was too small, rationalizing that you would lose weight and get into it eventually? What happened to that suit? You never got to wear it. Just because something looks good and has beautiful potential doesn't make it a wise investment. You end up losing in the end because it's just not a good fit.

One of the hardest things I ever had to do was accept the fact that the supposed man of my dreams would have robbed me of my destiny. If I had married him, you wouldn't be reading this book right now. I would be caught up in a whole different world, one that I thought I enjoyed, but one that wouldn't have helped me fulfill God's purpose for me. Therefore, inevitably, somewhere down the line a void would have become apparent in my life and caused problems between the two of us. I probably would not have been able to locate exactly what the problem was, so he would have absorbed the blame. This is where most couples end in divorce.

It took me a while to notice that though I had a good time

with this guy, he did not celebrate my gifts unless they benefitted him. As for me, I tucked this little footnote from the Holy Spirit away. I was in love, and that was all that mattered. So God saw fit to intervene and guide me back onto the right track. I have to admit that I was none too happy with my Savior for a while; I went back to the Lord wailing and screaming.

Yet today I can truly say that I am oh, so grateful. I celebrate the protection of God. I now know what I didn't know then: There is nothing like being smack-dab in the center of God's purpose for your life. You see, everyone who is good to you is not necessarily good for you—or for your God-ordained life design. Marriage is not about just you, or your personal desire to be loved and cherished. Marriage, from God's point of view, is all about effective partnerships for the sake of fulfilling kingdom business. Our personal pleasure just happens to be the automatic side effect of being in the center of God's will. So keep the big picture in mind as you analyze this next feature.

GIFTS AND ACCESSORIES

Does this man have a vision for his life? Is he running with that vision? Remember, God decided Adam needed help once Adam got busy *doing* his assignment. As we saw with Adam, a man doesn't need help until he is busy doing what he was created and called to do.

Please note that there is a clear distinction between having a God-given dream and your own personal agenda. Is your guy guided by a sense of destiny and purpose, or does he just allow life to happen around him? A man who is not certain of his mission can be a most miserable person—and you'll be miserable too if you know where *you* want to go in life.

A man who has a vision is not intimidated by a woman whose mission statement is clear. He is saturated by a sense of purpose and knows he will eventually get where he is going. A man who has a vision, and knows that God is backing him, can celebrate your gifts and see how they complement his. He will be your best ally, cheerleader, and assistant because he wants you both to make it!

It is imperative to place yourself where you and your gifts are celebrated, not tolerated. A man who cannot be a supporter of your achievements because he is floundering in a sea of uncertainty over his own life is not a healthy partner to have and to hold forever.

If you find yourself drawn to such a man—maybe you love being needed—resist the temptation to nurse this man to health or to mother him. You will lose yourself in the mix and gain his disdain. He already has a mother. He can pay for health care. You want to be a friend, a wife, and a lover, in that order. A friend allows the other the room to rise or fall on his own merit.

Usually, when we try to be all things to a man, we are acting from fear. Creating dependencies or feelings of obligation is not the way to get the best out of your man. Somewhere along the way he will resent you and flee from the smothering burden of obligation he associates you with.

No, girl, you want a man who is firmly anchored in his identity in Christ. Remember, we are looking for a man who will be priest and leader of his home. He, like Abraham, should be able to chart the direction for his family and lead it toward apprehending the promises of God. Like Jacob, he should want to roll obstacles from your path and do whatever it takes to win your hand. Like Boaz, his first instinct should be to want to cover you, redeem you, and provide for you. Your job is to decide if this is the man God has ordained for you to complement.

NO ROMANCE WITHOUT FINANCE

Now, what about your talents? Do your gifts complement his? Do his gifts complement yours? What about your temperaments? Do you see the two of you as an effective team capable of bringing blessing to the lives of those around you? Do your futures mesh? Can you coordinate your gifts in an attractive and effective way?

This is why knowing your purpose is so important. If your heart burns to go to the remote mission field, a rock star from Los Angeles, as cute and exciting as he may be, would not be the man for you. Make sure your hearts beat for mutual causes.

When I go shopping I always consider the fabric, the fit, and what I already have in my closet. Will my next purchase be a complementary addition to what I already have? If I find that I am going to have to buy shoes and matching accessories to go with a new outfit, I leave it right on the rack. It is too expensive a proposition.

If the man you meet makes you feel that you need to completely reinvent yourself, something is wrong. This is where I ask you to consider the relationship in terms of cost. Is this relationship expensive spiritually, emotionally, or physically? Does your longing for a mate make you willing to forfeit who you are in the process? Or does he see you as the gift that you are?

After all, he is the one who has found a "good thing." He is getting ready to step into an entirely new season of favor from the Lord because of what you bring into his life! I believe there is a dimension of favor that a man is unable to achieve until he has a suitable helpmeet, because a wife equips him to operate on a higher level than ever before. The man in your life should consider you a rare find, a priceless jewel—because of you he is getting ready to get blessed big-time!

Look at Scripture: "When Jacob saw Rachel daughter of Laban, his mother's brother, and Laban's sheep, he went over and rolled the stone away from the mouth of the well and watered his uncle's sheep. Then Jacob kissed Rachel and began to weep aloud" (Genesis 29:10–11).

Well, mercy me! That's what I'm talking about: a man who weeps in gratitude because he has found the one his heart has been searching for. The day my sister, Nicole, got married, her husband wept from the moment she began her walk down the aisle. After the wedding was over we asked him why he had cried. His response? "I couldn't believe how blessed I was. I kept thinking to myself, *She's all mine.*" What a man!

This runs in the family. When my cousin Jacqueline got married, her husband started weeping before the ceremony! There wasn't a dry eye in the house by the time she reached the altar. Again, here was a man who had no shame in confessing what a blessing he felt he had acquired. Two wonderful men, who were God's gifts in their own right, felt gifted by the presence of these women in their lives.

Girlfriend, any relationship that causes you to feel unworthy, unlovely, unacceptable, undesirable, or that you have to work for love, is too expensive. God has called the man to cover, protect, and provide not only materially for a woman, but emotionally and spiritually as well. You should be richer in mind, body, and spirit for your union with the man of your dreams.

You must understand that your heart is a valuable commodity. No one should be allowed access to it who doesn't understand its value. The man in your life should make rich deposits into your heart and spirit, not withdrawals.

And the love of God should be made more apparent to you in courtship and marriage. Though as a single you can understand God's love profoundly, this next level of intimate relationship should take you to a new experience of God's care for you. After all, these are the arms that God has chosen to be the physical manifestation of his love for you.

God gives clear instruction to men as to their role in a relationship: "Husbands, love your wives, just as Christ loved the church and gave himself up for her…. Husbands ought to love their wives as their own bodies. He who loves his wife loves himself" (Ephesians 5:25, 28).

Of course, a man can achieve this only if he has a healthy love and acceptance of himself. Hurting people hurt other people. It's a vicious cycle. Perhaps this is why a woman who meets a man who has just come out of a painful relationship usually doesn't fare well when it comes to securing a commitment. This is called the Transitional Woman Syndrome. The transitional woman usually doesn't make it to the altar. If she does, the backlash from being a man's rebound relationship can be excruciating. Make sure the man in your life has taken the time to heal from past relationships and has made peace with himself. How he cares for himself is how he will care for you.

Again, a man's relationship with God is crucial here. His love for himself will only be as strong as his love for God. This is not something that you can impart. You cannot be his Savior or his Teacher. That is out of spiritual order. In his rightful place as your personal priest, he should be leading you to a richer relationship with Christ. If he is causing you to compromise your faith and destabilize your walk, if he is leading you into sexual sin or causing you to be distracted from your commitment to Christ, the relationship is too expensive. Offending the Lover of your soul, who promises you eternal love, is too high a fare to pay for a ride that has a limited run.

It astounds me that nature knows more than humans do. Consider the female eagle. Before mating she tests the male to see if he can soar. As you know, most birds flap their wings in order to fly, but the eagle simply extends its massive wings and soars. It rides the current of the wind. So the female eagle flies higher and higher in the sky to make sure the male is capable of ascending heights.

This is an important test also because of eagles' mating practices. When they decide to procreate, they complete an intricate love flight, climbing higher and higher into the sky, where they lock talons and embrace in lovemaking while plummeting downward. If they don't start high enough, they will crash and die.

I think the symbolism is clear. If you and your man can't soar in the Spirit, when the force of your love for one another is tested by the pull or gravity of the world, your union will not be able to survive.

The female eagle performs another telling test. Once she sees that the male can soar, she rises even higher and begins dropping branches, one by one, heavier and heavier, to see if he can catch them. You see, she knows that if he cannot bear the weight of the sticks, he won't be able to build them a nest! Even the female eagle knows the male is responsible for preparing a place for her—namely, a house.

So you decide. How much is your life worth? How much is your love worth? You will be able to accept only what you believe you deserve. God himself calculated the worth of your love and decided it was worth his life. He now pledges you his love for eternity. Yes, Jesus set the example for all others to follow when he paid a ransom for his bride. Should you expect less from a mortal man?

Throughout the biblical age men were willing to pay the cost for the hand that they desired. The truth of the matter is, everyone knows that anything worth having costs. And no one gets a ride in this life for free.

So don't get on a bus that's headed in the wrong direction, girl. Relax in the certainty of God's wise provision, and enjoy the scenery from his arms.

Dear Heavenly Father, I confess that I have not always been as careful as I should have been with my heart. From time to time, my desire for love has caused me to leave my heart in the wrong hands. I now commit my heart into your hands for safekeeping.

Please help me to stop being so impulsive with what you deem so precious. As I learn to celebrate your love for me, let me learn from your example what a bridegroom should really be like. Help me to never settle for less than what you desire for me.

As I embrace you as the Lover of my soul, keep my affections in the haven of your own heart. As I rest in your love, make me more discriminating of those who approach me. I ask that you take over this area of my life. Keep me from those who have ungodly intentions toward me. Protect me from those you know would hurt my heart. I invite you to set a hedge around me and keep me from all who would draw me into unfruitful relationships until the day you present me to the mate that you have selected for me.

Grant me the discernment to recognize him as he recognizes me. Cleanse me from the temptation to typecast the men I meet according to what I see. Help me to trust in your knowledge and lean not to my own understanding. I know that you know what is best for me; therefore I yield to your choice, in Jesus' name. Amen.

EIGHT

ALL IS "FARE" IN LOVE

A wife of noble character who can find?
She is worth far more than rubies.

PROVERBS 31:10

In the interest of being fare, er, *fair,* since I've described what kind of bus you should be on the lookout for, I must address where you need to be as a woman in order to catch that bus. You didn't think I was just going to pick on the men, did you? Mm-mm, I'm an equal opportunity writer.

We've got to make sure you are a "good thing." We can't have that man calling God a liar once you get hold of him. We want the same reaction Eve got from Adam in the Garden: "The man said, 'This is now bone of my bones and flesh of my flesh'" (Genesis 2:23).

Adam was excited! He recognized Eve as his perfect mate right away. He didn't hold back how he felt about her. She didn't have to help him come to the conclusion that she was "it" for him. He instinctively knew and embraced her as his wife. And Adam loved him some Eve, so much so that he willfully followed her into sin in order not to be separated from her. There was something about Eve that evoked a strong emotional response from Adam.

WOMAN, WOMAN

We know from Genesis 2:25 that the man and the woman were both naked and unashamed. I believe Eve was unapologetically feminine. She was a woman and made no bones about it (pardon the pun). She was soft; she was warm. Her voice was like music. Everything about her was inviting to Adam. I'm sure she expanded his thinking, his way of looking at things, because of her own unique insights into the things she saw around her. She was completely herself, with no pretense.

And because of this, Adam found himself drawn to her. The first thing noted after they were expelled from the Garden tells us that: "Adam lay with his wife Eve, and she became pregnant and gave birth to Cain. She said, 'With the help of the LORD I have brought forth a man'" (Genesis 3:1).

The first thing Adam did was make love to Eve. Maybe he did this to solidify their covenant to one another; maybe to make amends. Maybe they needed to draw comfort from one another. Whatever the reason, it's plain to see that in spite of Eve's serious mistake, Adam still loved and desired her. So much for the need to be perfect in a man's eyes! When he loves you, he loves you.

Still, the right foundation must be laid. We have seen the danger of taking the lead. So my first question to you is: Are you willing to follow your man—spiritually, emotionally, and physically? Are you willing to follow his lead?

Imagine you are Sarah, and Abraham walks into your tent one morning and says, "Baby, we're moving." You ask where and he answers, "I don't know exactly; I'm just gonna follow God until he says stop."

Well! Are you willing to pack up that china and crystal, say good-bye to all your nearest and dearest, and follow this man off to God only knows where? Hopefully by now he's passed the fabric, fit, and financial test so you know that you can respect him and trust his judgment. But knowing all of that, are you willing to follow without putting in your two cents or holding up the show until God talks to you too? Because sometimes he won't.

Agreement is cool, but, girlfriend, sometimes God will test you in the submission department to see if you're still with him. Notice I said *with him,* not your husband. After all, submission is less about the man you're involved with and more about the God you follow. When you look at it in this light, you will see that submission is not passivity, it is a deliberate act of the will to walk in agreement with God. It is all about your making the choice to put yourself under God's covering, which puts you in a position to be protected and blessed.

FOLLOW THE LEADER

Sarah followed Abraham to the Promised Land. And Abraham insisted that the bride for Isaac be willing to follow too, to leave her home and come to where Isaac was. Abraham was cognizant of the fact that the Lord spoke to men about the direction for their families.

God spoke to Abraham about the generations to come in his family while Sarah was still barren. She, overhearing the conversation, laughed. Going one step further, she determined to help God fulfill his prophecy by giving her servant, Hagar, to Abraham. This proved only to complicate matters in the end. But in spite of fleshly mistakes, God's promise came to pass just as he had spoken it to Abraham.

Remember that the promise will lie in the man. Jesus was the promise. A woman conceived and birthed him, but the promise was revealed in his life and actions. In order for you to claim the promise once you've entered into a marriage, you must follow your husband's lead. If you've done your homework before you say "I do," you will have settled this issue before you have to put it into practice.

Remember, the friendship stage is where you check out his decision-making skills. Decide then if this man is unselfish, sensitive to the needs of others, and wise about the choices he makes. If you progress to courtship, you will be free to follow him to the marriage altar without looking back.

BEHIND EVERY GREAT MAN...

Part of being a good wife is having the ability to set up your husband for success. This involves respecting his thoughts, nurturing his dreams, applauding his accomplishments great and small, and caring for the things that are important to him. Check out the Word: "Her husband has full confidence in her and lacks nothing of value. She brings him good, not harm, all the days of her life" (Proverbs 31:11–12).

Another translation says, "She will not hinder him but help him all her life" (NLT). After all, you were created to help a man. A helper assists someone in being better than he was on his own. Girl, this means get over yourself! Marriage is not about what any one party can *get*. It's about what both parties have to *give*. Remember, God's definition of love is based on giving because he *gave* as proof of his love for us.

What type of woman are you? Rebekah went beyond the call of duty when Abraham's servant asked her for a drink at the well.

> "Drink, my lord," she said, and quickly lowered the jar to her hands and gave him a drink.
>
> After she had given him a drink, she said, "I'll draw

water for your camels too, until they have finished drinking." So she quickly emptied her jar into the trough, ran
back to the well to draw more water, and drew enough for
all his camels. Without saying a word, the man watched
her closely to learn whether or not the LORD had made
his journey successful. (Genesis 24:18–21)

Now, perhaps watering camels is not your style, but remember, when someone asks you for a favor, you never know who is
watching and why. Abraham's servant was bride shopping for his
master's son, Isaac. He was looking for a woman who had a servant's heart on top of all her other good features. Rebekah fit the
bill. She understood the value of a man's camels. She had a spirit
of hospitality and knew how to honor her guest. Watering camels
was no small task! Yet she happily embraced the job at hand.

This arduous task earned her some fabulous gold jewelry and
a very wealthy husband who loved and adored her all her days.
'Nuff said about being willing to serve.

Abraham's servant, Eliezer, determined she was a suitable
helpmeet for Isaac. This brings up another interesting question.
Are you equipped to be a helper, or are you looking for help? I find
it interesting that every single woman in Scripture who was spot-
ted by her mate was doing something productive, something fruitful. Rebekah was drawing water from a well. Rachel was watering
her father's flocks. Ruth was gleaning in the fields. The
Shulammite woman was tending the vineyard.

These were activities that nurtured life. These women culti-
vated the ingredients for communion. They were women who had
skills to bring to a household. They were not looking to be res-
cued, they were busy embracing the responsibilities of their present lives.

I always ask single women who are bemoaning their fate in

life: Do you simply want a husband, or do you want to be a wife? Be honest. If you dream only of knight on a white horse coming to carry you away, your vision is off-kilter. God decided to make a helper who was suitable for Adam. That means she was equipped to *add to* Adam's life, equipped to make Adam better and more effective and more prosperous than he already was. That is a powerful position.

My sister, you have the ability to make or break a man, so use your influence wisely. Remember—after you bake a cake, you get to eat it along with those you serve, but if you ruin the recipe, everyone is left hungry.

SEPARATING THE WOMEN FROM THE GIRLS

Consider the virtuous woman of Proverbs 31. Several statements stand out from this chapter. I will repeat my favorite because it is important to completely understand this: "Her husband has full confidence in her and lacks nothing of value. She brings him good, not harm, all the days of her life" (Proverbs 31:11–12).

The American Standard translation says, in my paraphrase, "his heart trusts in her." She had earned his trust and confidence. A woman sets the tone for this even before marriage by maintaining her purity. Purity is the outward show of inner self-control. A man needs to know that his woman can keep herself. Within the context of their relationship, he needs to know that she can keep the things concerning him as well. This is the call of every woman.

Because of the virtuous woman's track record, her husband felt that she always had his best interest at heart. Because of her he lacked nothing of value. What is valuable in a man's life? The security of a sound home, peace of mind in his surroundings, physical comfort, sexual fulfillment, productivity, accomplishment, and right standing with God. A woman can assist in all of these areas.

"She does him good and not harm"—she does not do things that threaten his security or self-worth. She does not run him into debt or make him look bad in front of his peers. She does not tear him down; she builds him up.

Remember, a man falls in love based on the way he feels when he is with you. To destroy his ego, nag him to death, criticize, and emasculate a man is not the way to secure the relationship, keep a tight leash on him, or whip him into shape. But it is a sure way to destroy your own—and his—happiness. As a matter of fact, it is downright foolish: "The wise woman builds her house, but with her own hands the foolish one tears hers down" (Proverbs 14:1).

Remember, if you belittle your man, your little man will be a mess of your own making. Your disposition as well as your physical handiwork in your home will directly affect your husband. And what affects him ultimately affects you. The atmosphere of a house is truly ruled by the woman. She sets the mood of her home and everyone in it. Martha Stewart is making millions teaching women what they should already know—ways to make the home an oasis. Home should be a man's favorite place. That will be determined by you.

You know how you feel when you go to someone's home and the smell of good food greets you as you enter? The way to a man's heart is still through his stomach.

If you just wrinkled up your nose at that statement, it's time for you to get your act together. Ladies, men like women who can cook! This is a common complaint I hear from men I meet all over the country: "Why can't women cook anymore?" Remember, the first females in their lives cooked for them. Cooking becomes a built-in expectation from the time they followed their mothers around the kitchen.

And hey, not only did the virtuous woman cook, she mixed it up: "She is like the merchant ships, bringing her food from afar. She gets up while it is still dark; she provides food for her family" (Proverbs 31:14–15).

The merchant ships brought exotic things from faraway places. People hurried to the dock to see what new and exciting things they brought. Likewise, the virtuous woman didn't cook the same casserole over and over again; she experimented with different dishes. Her family anticipated dinnertime; they came to the table anxious to see what delicious concoction she had come up with.

When I was a child, my mother was determined to expose us to different cultures through food. I never knew what to expect for supper. One night it was Italian food, another Mexican, another Hawaiian, another West Indian cuisine. I have learned to cook a sampling of all of these different things, to the delight of my friends and, unfortunately, my own taste buds. So experiment. A well-rounded woman should always have a repertoire of recipes that she's mastered.

But cooking goes beyond the natural. You should also have spiritual fare to share. The Proverbs 31 woman rose early. In Scripture this activity is usually associated with seeking God for instruction before the rigors of the day became demanding. Because of the specially sensitive nature of a woman, I believe that God imparts a special word to women for their households if they take the time to seek him. Get in the habit now of listening to God and cultivating spiritual dishes to serve others. Be equipped to serve not only physical bread, but the bread of life to those around you.

Now, let's see. What else did she do? "She considers a field and buys it; out of her earnings she plants a vineyard. She sees that her trading is profitable" (Proverbs 31:16, 18). The virtuous woman was fiscally responsible. She made wise financial decisions and contributed to the welfare of her household. She was not a monetary drain on her husband. She made investments that caused them all to profit. In our terms, she brought something to the party!

Now, I know that not everyone is good with money matters. Some people have good earning power, but no sense of how to handle the money they have made. Some people may not have great earning power, but are gifted with budgeting and allocating. In the times in which we live, both members of a household should be able to work as cooperative partners toward the common welfare of their home. Whether you choose to be a stay-at-home mom, professional homemaker, or a career woman, your responsibility to be an asset, not a liability, to your mate is crucial. He should not have to kill himself to provide you with an extravagant lifestyle. Learn to be financially creative in order to live within the boundaries of a comfortable income that doesn't stress out either party.

Some habits you've developed as a single will have to be put to death. One, for most who have been on their own for a while, is living above your means. Most singles do not have their money matters together at all. They are living check to check, hoping someone will come along to rescue them and make their existence easier. Let me ask you this: Would you like to marry someone who had a whole lot of bills? Would you appreciate a man who expected you to help pay debts that he acquired long before you were in the picture?

Well, this thing works both ways, my sister. If marriage to a good man is what you're hoping for, I suggest you go on a buying fast and ask God to assist you in cleaning up your finances. Don't be a foolish virgin (Matthew 25:1–13), oblivious to budgeting for the future. The day will come upon you suddenly and find you scrambling to get it together. Prepare for the wedding feast. Get yourself together and have enough oil in your lamp. It will be difficult for a man to see you as a gift if you come to him burdened down with debt.

Think about it. Now is the time to apply yourself to becoming financially free, not just for him, but also for yourself. Debt is bondage. Get rid of it!

IN SHAPE FOR THE PART

What else did she do? "She sets about her work vigorously; her arms are strong for her tasks" (Proverbs 31:17). I have the feeling that the virtuous woman was physically fit. Good physical health automatically translates to an abundance of energy and overall well-being. Especially in our stress-ridden age, exercise should be a part of everyone's daily routine. It is a great way to release tension and negative energy and equalize your emotions. When your body is sound, your mind is sound. When your body is fit, you won't buckle under pressure and exertion.

A sound body in good physical condition also heightens your self-confidence. When you look good, you feel good. Notice I haven't said that you should get in physical shape for a man—his attraction to you is just an added benefit. As you know, men are moved by what they see and even the most "saved" man you know wants an attractive woman by his side. So it won't hurt you to make the best physical presentation possible.

I am well acquainted with the fight for weight control. I spent the first half of my life severely underweight. As I began to gain, I panicked and began the cycle of dieting. I have been on most diet programs that you can name, from the Diet Center to Jenny Craig to Weight Watchers to the Rice Diet, the Cabbage Diet, the Beverly Hills Diet…. Whew! Are you tired yet? Or did all that talk about dieting make you hungry?

I've got to tell you, I just about lost hope that I would ever handle this weight thing. And that was my problem: It was all about me. I was trying to get my body under control instead of giving the control of my body back to God. Now I am gaining the victory daily through submitting my body daily to my first Husband,

Jesus Christ. Got it? As I seek to please him by no longer loving food more than him, he honors me by granting me a slim body. As the weight fell off, I gained a new appreciation for the body I had been given, and my self-esteem soared. And girl, the better I felt about myself, the more appreciative stares I got from buses passing by! I was free to be the beautiful woman my heavenly Father had created me to be.

I realize that weight loss is often more complicated than in my experience, but the principle is still true: Jesus deserves more love than my food does. And giving him that love makes me a freer, happier, more attractive woman.

This is the Lord's hope for every woman. If I can get there, so can you. Something happens when you feel good about yourself. You feel the need to make others feel good too.

This brings us back to the virtuous woman. "She opens her arms to the poor and extends her hands to the needy" (Proverbs 31:20). As singles we have the wonderful opportunity to utilize the abundance of time we have for the sake of others. Yet most of us remain self-centered, too busy murmuring over our fate in life. If this attitude doesn't change before marriage, trust me, it won't change after it either. Selfishness is a hard habit to break. It just bleeds into whatever situation we find ourselves in.

The virtuous woman was not selfish. She thought of the needs of others. She stretched beyond her comfort zone to extend compassion and help to others. She was civic minded. She was well rounded. Her life reached beyond her house in a way that brought balance to her world. She did not isolate herself. At the end of the day she had more to talk to her husband about than how crazy the kids drove her that day.

This woman applied the same gifts she utilized at home to bless others outside it. This set a good example for her children, inspiring them to have hearts of service. It brought respect to their house, as they were seen as a family with a heart for community outreach.

Check this out: "She is clothed with strength and dignity; she can laugh at the days to come" (Proverbs 31:25). Do you live in fear of the future? It is time to get on top of your circumstances. The Proverbs 31 woman was of sound character. She carried herself well. She was sober about the realities of life and readied herself and her family for them. The core of her being was anchored in the understanding of her purpose as a woman, a wife, a mother. She rose to the occasion and planned for the seasons of her life. She was not rocked by the unexpected twists and turns of life. She lived on the offense, anticipating the future. Physically, financially, spiritually, and emotionally, she was prepared.

She did not ride an emotional roller coaster. Understanding her strengths and her limitations, she took each day as it came. She had established her priorities and applied herself to what was truly important—her family members. Through it all she made it her business to be in tune with them and cognizant of all that went on in her household.

This is of vital importance when you consider the age in which we live. Children are under more pressure than ever before. Taking the time to talk and understand the hearts of your children and your mate can be a life-saving measure. And this is another benefit of those early morning talks with the Lord—he will fill in the blanks that your husband and children leave empty. He'll let you know what's really going on with them and prepare you to meet their needs daily. This keeps you on top of your household instead of grappling to slap on Band-Aids after the fact.

"She watches over the affairs of her household and does not eat the bread of idleness" (Proverbs 31:27). Part of making your husband's heart secure is being able to keep his house in order. The house you make will be a reflection of his ability to provide for you.

It will make a statement about who you are to his peers. Now is the time to establish the disciplines of homemaking and hospitality. This has to be the most underappreciated profession in society, yet it is most noticeable when it is not mastered. This is a routine that should be a part of your life now.

Look at it this way: your present home is his preview of his future with you. Take the time now to learn about the touches that will make your abode an oasis, a place a man would want to hurry back to. Learn how to set the atmosphere for peace and romance, comfort and security. A house doesn't become a beautiful sanctuary without work. But the effect it has on others is well worth it.

The virtuous woman even paid special attention to her bedroom: "She makes coverings for her bed; she is clothed in fine linen and purple" (Proverbs 31:22). She covered her and her husband's intimacy and protected her man's secrets. This is *sooo* important! This can cultivate or destroy your romantic life with your husband. Men hate being discussed with their wives' friends. They do not like their hearts to be exposed. They do not like all of their business in the streets.

A man needs to know that he has your confidence completely and that he can deposit the things that are close to his heart into your hands for safekeeping. A man needs to know he can lay his troubles down with you and not be criticized or made a public spectacle. He needs your special brand of ministry.

I find it interesting that the virtuous woman wore linen. Linen was what priests wore. Purple is the color of royalty and authority. This woman ministered to her husband while remaining covered in his authority. She fed his spirit and nurtured his dreams. She served him, loved him, and paid attention to the needs of his heart as well as his body.

Her words were well chosen. She was cognizant of the fact that the fruit those words would bear in his life would ultimately affect her: "She speaks with wisdom, and faithful instruction is on her tongue" (Proverbs 31:26).

The man in your life should be able to seek your encouragement and inspiring insights and find it. You are called to keep his secrets and dispel his fears; to weigh his thoughts and gently bring clarity to his world. And when you don't know what else to say, you simply listen and pray.

The instruction you give to him should be consistently edifying. Your conversation should be seasoned with grace and sensitivity and always give life.

I can hear some of you saying, "But what about him?" I say, what *about* him? We're talking about you and what God has called you to be in the life of a man. As you love and serve him as unto the Lord, his response will be all the things you are longing for. But you must keep in mind God's bottom line.

> The woman is the glory of man. For man did not come from woman, but woman from man; neither was man created for woman, but woman for man.
>
> In the Lord, however, woman is not independent of man, nor is man independent of woman. For as woman came from man, so also man is born of woman. But everything comes from God. (1 Corinthians 11:7–9, 11–12)

Yes, everything comes from God, even the order of marriage and the order of authority. We are all called to submit to one another. It is important to allow the man in your life to be the man, the leader, the priest God has called him to be. Your life as a woman will be easier when you live it by God's design.

Of course, it is ultimately easier to submit to a husband who is submitted to God. His love for you will inspire your heart to do what your head rebels against. But no matter what, we must be the women that God has designed us to be. Only then can he move in our defense.

This brings me to the bottom line of this whole exercise: "Charm is deceptive, and beauty is fleeting; but a woman who fears the LORD is to be praised" (Proverbs 31:30). Being the type of woman a bus wants to stop for comes from living in the fullness of a thriving relationship with God. What is going to separate you from all the other women standing on the corner? Your countenance. Your spirit. We all know and understand that men are moved by what they see. But it takes more to make them come to a full stop. If you want a godly man, something will be required of you. The godly man that you are seeking is looking for a godly woman. He isn't seeking one who has a convenient Christianity—one who knows all the lingo but lives life in a carnal fashion. No, he is looking for a woman he can trust. You're looking for a man you can trust. How will you know that you can trust one another? By seeing how accountable you are to God. That's where the rubber meets the road.

That is the only constant. A person who is accountable to God treats others in accordance with his Word. That promises a rich, full relationship, one filled with consideration, love, and trust.

When you get down to it, being physically beautiful is where it only begins. Trusting in the outer trappings will get us just so far down the road. Why? Because perfection is so subjective. Pursuing it can lead to obsession and bondage if you don't discover the secret of true beauty: a pure heart, a sweet spirit, and a soul that is wholly surrendered to God. These are powerful magnets.

Jesus, the ultimate Bridegroom, will come looking for a specific bride: one who is radiant, without stain or wrinkle or any blemish, holy and blameless (Ephesians 5:27). Man, made in his image, reflecting his spiritual virtue, seeks the same thing. As you live to please the Lover of your soul, you will automatically attract your physical lover.

So as one famous preacher would say, "Get ready, get ready, get ready!" Without and within, get ready. Make the outside the best that it can be. That may not necessarily be a size six, but the size that makes you feel good about you. Prepare your arms to serve, your lips to speak with grace, your heart to constantly pour out streams of refreshing, and your eyes to constantly reflect the love of God that burns within.

On that note, you won't even have to wait at the corner for that bus to come along. As you continue walking toward the One who loves you most, that bus will stop and offer you a ride!

Dear Heavenly Father, you are the Potter, I am the clay. I submit myself to your hands. Fashion, make, and mold me into a vessel of blessing for the man that you've prepared me for. Help me to help him and not hinder him all the days of my life.

Continue to complete the work that you've begun in me that I might be a "good thing" in his life. Let my touch always be healing, my words always inspiring, my love always intoxicating.

Help me to have a spirit of prayer, that my discernment may be keen, and my contributions always timely.

Teach my hands to work diligently and eagerly. Grant me a giving heart. Let my lips be ruled by wisdom, discretion, and prudence.

Touch my spirit, and make me sensitive to the needs of the man that you place in my life.

But most of all, dear Lord, while I am waiting, help me to be a vessel of honor for you, a reflection of your splendor and your grace. Help me to walk in the liberty of being a woman by your design, to embrace my femininity as a priceless gift and rejoice in it.

Let my joy be a blessing to others around me. May I remember at all times that I was first created for your pleasure, your glory, and your love. Amen.

NINE

DESTINATION: LOVE CITY

He has taken me to the banquet hall, and his banner over me is love.
SONG OF SOLOMON 2:4

Now that you're in the right place at the right time, doing the right thing, reaching your ultimate destination still hinges on one important factor. Keeping your goal in sight is crucial once you begin your bus ride.

It's important that you know the landmarks along the way. Have you ever set off on a trip, and the farther you went, the more unfamiliar the scenery became? That was your indication that you were going the wrong way. Well, in order to know if you are on the right bus, headed in the right direction, you've got to visit Love City long before you try to accompany another person there. You've got to know what love looks like! And believe me, it doesn't look like the movies. It is not combustible, changeable, manipulative, deceitful, secretive, or selfish. No, no.

Love is patient, love is kind. It does not envy, it does not boast, it is not proud. It is not rude, it is not self-seeking, it is not easily angered, it keeps no record of wrongs. Love does not delight in evil but rejoices with the truth. It always protects, always trusts, always hopes, always perseveres.

Love never fails. (1 Corinthians 13:4–8)

If you're riding a bus right now and you haven't seen any humble landmarks, no thoughtful, patient, or kind monuments, you need to get a transfer—quick. You are not on the way to love—that bus is going somewhere else. If you persist in holding on to your seat, you better believe that bus is going to break down.

But the right kind of love, God's kind of love, never, ever fails! It doesn't fail when someone cuter comes along. It doesn't fail when there's a misunderstanding. It doesn't fail when "the thrill is gone," because it's not based on externals. With true love there is no need for chemistry because the heart burns on supernatural energy fueled by the Master Chemist himself. Love endures because it is not something. Love is Someone! As we embrace him and his love for us, he then dwells in us, giving us the capacity to love others with his heart. This is why, after all is said and done about catching buses, you'd better be caught up in a serious love affair with the Bus Driver. And that makes perfect sense since he is the one whose hands are on the wheel!

It saddens me to think of how many brush away the arms of the Lover of their souls in their pursuit of the love of a natural man, only to watch that man drop their hearts and break them into a million pieces. Then we come back with our broken offerings to lay before the Master. He lovingly scoops up all the fragments, ministers to our spirit, and restores our heart just in time for us to snatch it back out of his hands and run off after yet another undeserving lover. How do we stop the cycle of painful relationships in search of the perfect mate? I've said it before, but it's still true.

> Delight yourself in the LORD and he will give you the desires of your heart. (Psalm 37:4)

> But seek first his kingdom and his righteousness, and all these things will be given to you as well. (Matthew 6:33)

> You need to persevere so that when you have done the will of God, you will receive what he has promised. For in just a very little while, "He who is coming will come and will not delay." (Hebrews 10:36–37)

> Keep yourselves in God's love as you wait for the mercy of our Lord Jesus Christ to bring you to eternal life. (Jude 1:21)

WHEN I FALL IN LOVE

Keeping yourself and your heart hidden in the love of God is for your own safety. As you embrace the notion of his being your first and greatest Love, you will be set free from the bondage of loneliness. Yes, the Lord God himself is the first Man you need to be head over heels in love with. Choosing to delight yourself in the Lord invites him to lavish you with his love and attention in a way you've never known. This will provide you with a standard of love against which you can measure those in pursuit of your hand.

I am so glad I prayed that dangerous prayer years ago. You know, the one where I challenged God not to give me a mate until he could prove to me that I could be happy with just him. Well, he has done it! And what a romance it has been! He has kept me surrounded by blessings and evidences of his love for me, so much so that the other day I had to ask him a hypothetical, yet very important question.

"Lord," I said, "when I get married, are you going to continue to spoil me the way you do now, or are you going to back off a bit to give my husband a spot to fill?" I needed to know this before I decided my disposition toward marriage. I was not relishing the thought of giving up the good life I had been enjoying.

As I was mulling over how much my life had changed since I had made the decision to really pursue a love relationship with God, I had a vision. I was standing in the middle of a church aisle in my wedding dress. The Lord was standing at the back of the church, at the beginning of the aisle. My fiancé awaited me at the altar. I stood between them, looking back and forth, unable to decide which direction to take. Finally, I went to the back of the church and took the Lord's hand and proceeded down the aisle. When I reached the front, I joined the hand of the Lord with the hand of my husband. I heard the Lord say to me, "I'll come if you invite me."

How do you get to the place where you have nourished such passion with God that you can't bear to be apart from him? How do you get to the place where you, like David, say, "Do not cast me from your presence or take your Holy Spirit from me" (Psalm 51:11)? Take my husband, take my job, take my wardrobe, just don't leave me, God! The thought of living without you is too dark and dismal a thought.

Not many people can say that. They say they love God, but they say it without feeling. They actually "love" him from Christian duty, from fear of not being blessed, but they don't *love* him with their hearts. There is a big difference.

I believe this is a difficult concept for many singles to grasp because God seems far away. God is up there and we are down here. He is the Mighty One. We don't dare think of reducing him to earthly terms—a Man with a heart who desires to have an intimate romance with us. And yet, though he is not mere man, he does desire to have a passionate love affair with us, his Bride. And he doesn't want it to be a long-distance relationship, either.

CROSSING THE GREAT DIVIDE

Let me tell you a story. A few years ago while in Africa I met a dashing man who lived in Paris—he was part French, don'tcha know. We clicked and made plans for the future. I was to learn French so I could converse with his friends; he was to finish getting his master's degree in architecture and join me in the States; and we would live this very exciting, transcontinental life. Doesn't that just sound marvelous?

Well, after several months of phone calls and faxes and delays in his master's program, boyfriend ran out of steam. One day I received a letter in the mail. It informed me that he could no longer tolerate our long-distance relationship. It seems he needed a tangible girlfriend, one he could see and touch. So though he would always "treasure my friendship" (right!), he believed we should part company.

Get the point? Relationships must be nurtured. They require quality time in which the partners can discover one another in new ways daily. Exchanging needs and intimacies is crucial to the existence and furtherance of a love union.

Since neither my Frenchman nor I was willing to move from our personal comfort zone for the sake of the other, obviously we did not love one another enough to work at securing our relationship. We are often like this with God.

Are you having a long-distance relationship with God? Do you ignore him all week? Are you too busy to pray, yet you faithfully show up at church to see what the preacher has to say about God?

Do you run around to every meeting to get a word from God through speakers and prophets, yet still fail to draw near to God yourself?

Yet God has moved from his comfort zone several times in an effort to reach out to us and make our love relationship with him work. In the beginning he came down from heaven to walk and talk with man in the cool of the evening in the Garden of Eden. Think about that: God came down to visit with mere man. Now that's what I call a giant leap for mankind!

And when that fell through, God changed his approach a little. He still came down, but not as far. Man then had to show his interest by going up to meet with God. In Exodus 19 we find God coming down to the slopes of Mount Sinai to visit with the children of Israel. He came to let them know that he backed Moses as their leader and to give them his commandments. I believe God's first intention was always to speak to us directly instead of writing anything down. He came to give the Israelites the Ten Commandments in person! But they became overwhelmed by his awesome presence, drew back in fear, and said they didn't want to have anything to do with God. They told Moses to be their spokesperson with God—they would hang back, thank you very much: "They trembled. They stayed at a distance and said to Moses, 'Speak to us yourself and we will listen. But do not have God speak to us or we will die'" (Exodus 20:19).

How sad. God loved these people in dramatic and life-altering ways, but their fear kept them from coming near him. It was at this point that God chose to begin writing letters to his people because they forfeited having direct conversation with him. They stood in the doorways of their tents and watched Moses go in to the Tent of Meeting; they watched the cloud descend and cover the tent once Moses was inside. They waited while Moses communed with God and watched as he came back out, his face all aglow from being in the presence of God. They worshiped from afar.

I'm here to tell you: That breaks God's heart. He wants you to come close! Sometimes I just sit and ponder how God felt when all of this was going on. His heart beat so passionately for his people that he steadfastly pursued them. So next he decided that if the people didn't want to come near to him, he would at least commune with the priests and elders. So in Exodus 24 God had Moses bring the seventy leaders he had selected, along with Aaron and his sons, to go up on Mount Sinai to visit with God. They all saw God. They even ate a meal in his presence! But it did not forge a relationship. It became merely a religious experience. How do I know? Because of what took place in Exodus 32. Moses went up to receive instructions from God, and meanwhile the people fell apart. By the time Moses made it back down the mountain, Aaron had helped the Israelites construct a golden calf to worship. That's what happens with religion.

"The Lord says: 'These people come near to me with their mouth and honor me with their lips, but their hearts are far from me. Their worship of me is made up only of rules taught by men" (Isaiah 29:13). This is God's definition of lip service, and many people practice it today. Many now eat in the presence of God, but never embrace him.

"But, Michelle, I thought we were talking about how to get a man!"

Oh, trust me, we are. The biggest secret to getting the kind of man you truly want is hidden in your relationship with Christ. You see, all of these people who never made the move to anchor their hearts in the Lord failed to receive the promise. These were the same people who had trouble believing they could inhabit the Promised Land. Why? Lack of relationship. When you don't have a relationship with someone, it is impossible to trust him. The only ones who believed that they could go in and possess the land were those who had experienced intimacy and heart relationships with God: Moses, Joshua, and Caleb. Not even the priests were able to believe because though they bore the title, religious people are unable to trust God. That's why they trust in works and fail miserably.

God called Moses his friend. Joshua lingered in the presence of God even after Moses left the Tent of Meeting (Exodus 33:11). And Caleb followed God wholeheartedly all of his life. They had embraced God! They knew him. They heard his voice. They trusted him because they could not be divorced from the evidence of his care for them or his mighty power.

Girlfriend, you won't have the faith it takes to embrace a natural relationship if you don't get to a place of intimacy with God. Believe me, relationships require faith.

Let's face it. Until you can get to the point where God and his will matter more to you than anything else, marriage is an idol, a god in your life. And guess what, people: God is not interested in blessing anything that divides your heart against him. We've said it before: He is a jealous God.

You shall have no other gods before me. (Exodus 20:3)

I am the Lord; that is my name!
     I will not give my glory to another or my praise to idols. (Isaiah 42:8)

But you have forsaken me and served other gods, so I will no longer save you. (Judges 10:13)

God will not intervene in all those painful relationships you insist on having if he is not first in your heart. He will allow man to disappoint you in order to show you the supremacy of his love and restoration. He will not share the part of his heart that he has reserved for himself with another man, especially one who cannot appreciate your love.

So smash the altar of marriage in your heart. The root of a wonderful love relationship on earth is hidden in your love relationship with the Lord. At the end of the day it is to him that you will go for the wisdom and strength to maintain a marriage. If you have no intimate relationship with him, how will you approach him? First things first: Fall in love with God.

THE LOOK OF LOVE

It's a funny thing about being in love. Suddenly you're more appealing than ever! Everyone wants someone who is in love already. I know you've experienced this. After a long drought of datelessness, you finally have started seeing someone. All of a sudden you have invitations coming out of the woodwork. You scratch your head and wonder, *Where were all these guys when I didn't have anyone?*

Ever notice what all singles say: "All the good ones are already taken"? Well, that's not true. I'm still out here; you're still out here; so all the good ones are not taken yet. Why do we say that? Because it seems that all the people who are spoken for have a certain attractive air about them. They exude a confident sense of self, an unspoken esteem, that is enticing. They are possessed by another, and they reflect a wholeness that comes from that.

Yet we can possess that same air if we see our relationship with the Lord in the same light. We are desired; we are spoken for; we are brides-to-be! That should change the way we walk and talk. That should do something to the air around us. Someone loves us fiercely and fervently. We are pursued! We are possessed! Our faces should glow like Moses' did when he came down the mountain after visiting with God. Others should be drawn to the light.

Yet we still avoid God and go in search of others. Why is this?

I think I know one reason. We don't like what having a true relationship with God requires: separation from some things and some people. Pursuing a love relationship with God calls for our spending time alone, seeking his face, listening for his insights into the intricate workings of our hearts and our lives. He wants to reveal some secrets to us; give us direction. Yet we shy away.

For one thing, we don't like spending time alone. If there's one thing singles have too much of, it's time alone! We're also afraid of what God might tell us. Then we might have to act on what he says. I know all about this because I've been there.

If we're truly honest, we admit that we want Jesus to come into our hearts and bless our mess. We get uncomfortable when he starts suggesting changes. When he tries to help us clean up some areas, we grow faint. This might sound mean, but girl, most Christians are just downright lazy. We take advantage of the grace factor in all the wrong ways. Religions of the world demand much more from their disciples. So while others crucify their flesh to appease a god who gives them nothing, we willfully abuse the kindness of the one and only true God who gives us everything.

We avoid prayer and find everything else to do. And when we finally do show up before the throne of grace, we come with a list of demands. What is wrong with this picture? We fail this way because like the Israelites, we do not understand the heart of the One who loves us most. We don't really hear his desire when he says to us, "Call to me and I will answer you and tell you great and unsearchable things you do not know" (Jeremiah 33:3).

God longs to commune with us and share his plans and his heart with us. Prayer is an opportunity to share what's on your heart, but it's also a time to find out what is on his; to weep over the things he weeps over; to rejoice over the things that make him smile; to put to death some issues; and to breathe life into others. As we learn more about God's heart, we will become more passionate toward him. Then prayer time takes on a whole new flavor: It becomes "get free" time! I never considered it as such until I fell in love with the Lord.

CORRECTING OUR VISION

I've already told you how I held a portion of my heart back from God on purpose for a long time. I was afraid that if I agreed to give him my whole heart, he would keep it and not allow me to share it with another. Isn't that silly? Yet many of us have these weird concepts of God.

It reminds me of the story of the merchant who, before leaving on a long journey, gave talents to his workers according to their abilities. When he returned, the one he had given five talents to had doubled his investments. The one with two had done the same. But the one who had been given one talent had messed up big-time.

> Then the man who had received the one talent came. "Master," he said, "I knew that you are a hard man, harvesting where you have not sown and gathering where you have not scattered seed. So I was afraid and went out and hid your talent in the ground. See, here is what belongs to you."
>
> His master replied, "You wicked, lazy servant! So you knew that I harvest where I have not sown and gather where I have not scattered seed? Well then, you should have put my money on deposit with the bankers, so that when I returned I would have received it back with interest.
>
> "Take the talent from him and give it to the one who has the ten talents." (Matthew 25:24–28)

Well, isn't that special? Here is the master being considerate enough to leave with each only what he knew each man could handle. He didn't wish to give them more responsibility than they could bear. He was willing to share the gain with those who constructively used what he had left, but what does he get for his kindness? Faithfulness on the part of two servants, but a heap of misunderstanding on the part of the third. The servant just decided that his master was not nice, not fair, not trustworthy, not generous, and therefore not worthy of any effort. This servant did not desire the increase and joy of his master. He felt his master had enough already—as a matter of fact, more than he was due!

Some of us feel this way about God. What about you? Do you think God is unfair in wanting to be your first love? Do you think he deserves less? Have you developed a perverted view of God's care for you? Do you feel he owes you something—that he must do something more to earn your love?

Like starving dogs who are thrown a bone, we require so little of a natural man when one comes into our lives. Why do we make God work so hard? He's made the first move and the last move. Jesus completely disconnected the concept of the long-distance relationship by coming from heaven to earth through the womb of a woman, in living flesh, to reclaim our love and close the gap between us and God. He has even sent us a Comforter and Keeper, the Holy Spirit, to dwell within us until he comes to take us to himself.

Girl, stop looking for a knight on a white horse. You've set your standards too low! There is a *King* coming, don'tcha know, on a white horse to carry us away (Revelation 19:11)! Jesus Christ has done all the work to deserve our love. It is time to stop giving it to those who do so much less.

As we turn our hearts toward the Lord, our countenance will change and color our world a whole different hue. Our perspective will change—life will be far more beautiful when seen through the eyes of loving him. That's when others will begin to notice the transformation and comment. That's when you will begin to attract a whole different type of man.

Yeah, this bus will be driving the right kind of route!

PREPARING FOR ARRIVAL

The other day I went to my voice agent's office to audition for a voice-over job. While I was preparing to read my lines, she was studying me. Finally she said, "Michelle, is there a man in your life?"

"No," I answered, "why do you ask?"

"Well," she said, "I haven't heard you mention or talk about a man in years, yet you always seem so happy. Your eyes are always lit up and you always have a smile on your face. So I was just wondering if there was something you weren't telling us."

I jokingly replied, "Perhaps that's why I'm so happy—because there's no man in my life making me crazy."

As I left her office I began to mull over our conversation. I started calculating when the last time was that I had a real love interest in my life. To my amazement, I realized it had been about seven years! Why, I hadn't even noticed the time racing by. Much had happened since that last failed romance. I had turned my attentions toward another Man. This man is truly a Renaissance Man. He does some of everything and does it all well. His specialty is law, but he also has a miraculous touch in the field of medicine. He is quite an artist, creating colors and sounds that cannot be duplicated. He is also an incredible therapist. After a session with him, the brokenhearted are made whole, and the bound are set free.

What's he like? Well, he comes from a good family—royalty, in fact. He is so handsome, he's the fairest of ten thousand. Faithful? He has promised to never leave me or forsake me. He's always available, no matter what time of day or night I call. I'm always his first priority. Romantic? He has written me the longest love letter in history—hundreds of pages. And the man has deep pockets, okay? The cattle on a thousand hills belong to him and he is willing to share all that he has with me. He promises to supply all of my needs according to the abundance of his riches.

I am so proud to belong to this Man because of his reputation. If I stood in the middle of any crowd and said his first name, everyone would know who he was. And he's not afraid of commitment. He's gone to prepare a place for me and make ready a banquet where he will introduce me to his father, who is a very important man. And yet with all of this going on, he is a perfect gentleman: he stands at the door and knocks. He never forces entry into my home. He patiently waits to be invited in. But the thing I love about him most is his generosity. He is so generous, he even gave his life for me.

What is his name? Wonderful, Counselor, Mighty God, Everlasting Father, the Prince of Peace. Jehovah Jireh, Jehovah Shalom, Jehovah Nissi, Jehovah Rapha, El Shaddai…oh, so many names. According to my heart and my need, I call him, but most of the time I simply call him Jesus. He is my everything, and I am totally his.

And so it is with a full heart that I expect to be found by a natural man, because to be caught up in a love affair with Jesus is to have nothing lacking in my world. For years I cringed when people told me that Jesus would be my husband. I wanted a physical touch. Little did I know that his touch went so much deeper. Truly he is able to satisfy completely and profoundly.

Girlfriend, fall in love with the Bus Driver first. Experience a tour of Love City so you'll know it the next time you see it. Then waiting for the bus itself will be easy.

On that note, I've got to go. I believe I see my bus coming around the corner. But that's another book! Tah-tah!

Dear Heavenly Father, forgive me for ignoring your arms. Forgive me for offering you crumbs from my heart. I have been mistaken in my pursuit of love, but it is with clearer vision that I turn back to you right now.

I ask you to teach me to love you the way that you love me. Make your love real to me and help me to joyfully embrace it. Grant me the joy of my salvation and the peace that you promise will be beyond my comprehension.

Help my heart to be constant, abiding in you, in spite of changing or unchanging circumstances. May your love keep me safe, secure, and warm. Hold me close to your heart and let me hear your heartbeat. Make my heart beat like yours.

Fill me with a passion for your Spirit, a thirst for your Word, and a hunger for your voice. I pray that you will be my constant craving, and as I wait for you to fill my longings, you will fill me completely with yourself to overflowing.

And last but not least, I ask that you will be my first and greatest love. In Jesus' name I pray. Amen.

Multnomah Publishers®

The publisher and author would love to hear your comments about this book. *Please contact us at:*
www.multnomah.net/ifmenarelike

RECOMMENDED READING:
What To Do until Love Finds You by Michelle McKinney Hammond
Secrets of an Irresistible Woman by Michelle McKinney Hammond
Knight in Shining Armor by P. B. Bunny Wilson
I Kissed Dating Goodbye by Joshua Harris
Choosing God's Best by Don Raunikar
The Lady, Her Lover, and Her Lord by T. D. Jakes
Opposites Attract by Tim & Beverly LaHaye
31 Secrets of an Unforgettable Woman by Mike Murdock

To correspond with Ms. McKinney Hammond, write to:
HeartWing Ministries
P.O. Box 11052
Chicago, Il. 60611

or e-mail her at: heartwingmin@yahoo.com
or visit her website at: mckinneyhammond.com or heartwing.com

For speaking engagement enquiries, contact:
Speak Up Speaker Services
1 (888) 870-7719

Ladies, be as determined to get information as you are to embrace anything that is important to you. If your local bookstores do not have these books in stock, they are always happy to order them for you. When all else fails, there's always Amazon.com. Happy reading!